Praise

"All I could think about while reading The Other "F" Word was "this is going to help so many people!" Written in a warm, sometimes witty, and completely honest way, the author's heart-wrenching story begins with a tragic loss that leads to unshakeable faith. This book is for anyone who could use a little extra courage to carry on."

—TERRI BURNETT

Founder, Executive Director, Women's Nonprofit Alliance

"Sara Stamp's story speaks to the rawness and realness of life. Her honest and authentic style of writing allows us to not only feel with her pain, but also learn from her heart how to grow in faith through our own personal struggles. No matter what you are walking through, Sara reminds us that we can discover joy and hope in the process."

—KAROL LADD

Bestselling author of The Power of a Positive Mom

"Sara Stamp gives God the glory He is due through the greatest heartache known to mankind, the loss of a child, her precious Layla. To walk through the valley of the shadow of death, clinging to Him throughout the journey is the beautiful story bravely shared through "The Other F-Word." Sara is a lifelong friend, amazing wife and mom, sister in Christ but most importantly a daughter of the King. May the hope she shares through her relationship with Jesus be a light to us all."

—MICHELLE HENDERSON

Children's Ministry Pastor, Bent Tree Bible Church

THE *other* F-WORD

THE other F-WORD

WHEN **FAITH** FILLS THE GAP

SARA STAMP

KAT BIGGIE PRESS

Columbia, SC

KAT BIGGIE PRESS
Columbia, SC

www.katbiggiepress.com

Printed in the United States of America
ISBN 978-1-948604-27-7

Library of Congress Control Number: 2019931552

Cover Design: Fresh Design

Author Photograph: Laura Potter

First Edition

10 9 8 7 6 5 4 3 2 1

To my angel Layla.
Thank you for teaching me that I can make my rainbows
any color I want.

"Expect great things from God; attempt great things for God."

~William Carey

Contents

Foreword

When my daughter Kathryn died just two days after she was born, my faith died with her. I was so angry, mostly at God. I felt like I had been abandoned in my greatest time of need.

I was also angry at the people in my life who said things like, "She's in a better place now," or "It was meant to be," or other platitudes that were meant to be comforting, but were ultimately very much the opposite. If you've ever lost a child, you probably heard some of these sentiments, and likely felt the same emotions that I felt when hearing them. I just wanted to scream, "The BEST place for her would be with her mother!" Or, "How could this much pain be God's plan?"

My anger resurfaced when I saw other mothers whose babies suffered from the same disease Kathryn and her sister had, Twin to Twin Transfusion Syndrome, but who were lucky enough to have both their children survive. I wasn't mad at the mothers or the babies, I was grateful for their lives. But I was mad at God for not saving my daughter and that my surviving daughter would grow up without her identical twin. I heard these other mothers say things like, "I prayed every day for our babies, and our prayers were answered."

Why weren't MY prayers answered? Why weren't my prayers good enough?

So in response, I shut God out. Because clearly, he wasn't listening to me. I used the "f" word a lot. But it wasn't Sara's other "F" word. It wasn't Faith. I was done with Faith.

Over the years, what I came to find out is that I wasn't abandoned. I was given everything I needed, and more, to survive our situation and then go on to positively impact and become a beacon of light for many other mothers who have also suffered the loss of a child. And as my anger faded, I began allowing faith back in. Only when I began to do that, did I truly begin to heal.

It's natural to be angry when you've lost a child. But Sara's beautiful book demonstrates that you can feel all of these emotions—you can be angry and disappointed, and even wonder why your prayers seemingly weren't answered—and still walk with God and have faith that he's holding you close.

It took a long time for me to come back. Some days I feel as though I'm still trying to make my way back to the trust and blind faith I had prior to Kathryn's death. But I know one thing for certain—faith makes it easier, even though faith itself is far from easy.

Sara Stamp and I met when her daughter was still in treatment. Sara was so optimistic and full of faith that sweet Layla would be cured. And it didn't happen. Some people would take the road I took and turn their back on their faith, at least for a short while. But not Sara. She immediately started writing. She immediately felt a need to share her faith with the hope of helping another person going through the same struggles. She has written an uplifting, at times even funny book that will reach deeply into your core and show you that true faith means following and accepting even when we are brought to our knees. True faith is accepting our battle wounds, accepting our scars, and turning towards God, not away, during our times of greatest sorrow. When you do this, when you allow the Holy Spirit to wrap around you and hold you tightly, you will find comfort.

Be warned, Sara's wit made me laugh out loud a few times in this book. It was unexpected and appreciated. I've always thought that laughter through tears is one of the greatest emotions we can have, and I appreciate her ability to tackle such a difficult subject while maintaining her beautiful sense of humor.

It's okay not to be strong after you've suffered a tremendous loss. It's okay to be angry and question everything. It's okay to have cracks and chinks in your armor. In "Anthem", Leonard Cohen's song about hope in the darkness, he declares that the cracks are where the light gets in. We all have cracks—just be sure to let the faith in.

Sara's beautiful book is about her journey through the loss of her precious child, but it's also packed with insights into how faith kept her moving forward. The Other 'F' Word is a wonderful tool for any broken heart, anyone wondering why or how this could have happened to them. Sara helps you realize that faith is not easy and having faith doesn't mean everything is going to work out like you hoped it would. But choosing to walk in faith will help lift the burden of all these things—anger, sadness, anxiety, fear—and help you find peace once more.

May Sara's words help you find encouragement, light, and faith in your healing.

Alexa Bigwarfe
Author, *Sunshine After the Storm: A Survival Guide for the Grieving Mother*

Founder, Sunshine After the Storm—a non-profit to support grieving mothers

Introduction

I became a mom when I was thirty-two years old. For a long time, I didn't know if I wanted to have kids. I secretly worried I wouldn't be any good at it. I've always been a stick-with-what-you-know gal and the thought of raising tiny humans seemed a little frightening. Would I know what to do? Would they like me? Would it be difficult? Yes. Yes. And Absolutely Yes. But the moment I looked into my little girl's eyes, with her mile-long eyelashes, I was in love. Layla Rose Stamp made me a new person in an instant.

Everyone thinks their kid is the most amazing kid (come on, ya know it's true), but I can say without a doubt in the world that Layla was something truly special. When she entered a room, it was in arms-out-wide style, with a booming Oprah-esque voice announcing "I'm heeeeeeeere!" And I mean that in every literal sense. No matter the audience, she was the main attraction. Her little brother Daniel was her personal lackey, following her everywhere and doing everything she said. She was kind, funny, and smart as a whip. My husband, Bryan, and I used to joke that she got his mouth and my brains, which would make her either a superhero or a super villain. Luckily for us, she only used her powers for good.

Life with our little family of four was great. We had fantastic friends, good jobs, and a comfortable home. That's not to say we didn't have our ups and downs, but we didn't have much to complain about in the way of real problems. That all changed on October 18, 2016—a day that will always be one of the worst days of our lives.

A few weeks after her fourth birthday, Layla began to complain about a sore neck and headaches. I brushed it off as sleeping wonky on her pillow until her symptoms began to get worse. Giving in to my gut feeling, I took her to the emergency room at our local children's hospital where I rattled off the list of symptoms to the nurses and doctors. With a concerned look, the ER doctor ordered a CT scan . . . and we waited.

We were shocked when the scan revealed a large mass in the back of Layla's skull. Within an hour we were in transit downtown to Children's Medical Dallas Center My husband and I were devastated and in complete disbelief.

Over the next six hours we spoke with countless physicians and nurses, signed more paperwork than when we bought our house, and put our sweet girl into the hands of strangers. Surrounded by family and friends, we prayed together as Layla underwent a five-hour surgery to remove the mass. Finally, the surgeon gave word that everything had gone as smoothly as possible. "Tomorrow you'll meet with the oncologist," she said. It was in this moment that reality set in—Layla had brain cancer.

It took weeks for Layla to regain gross motor functions and the ability to speak after the surgery. I spent hours on my knees praying to hear her voice. Never again would I take for granted hearing her squeaky voice ask me the same question over and over (and over and over). Slowly, and with a ton of hard work, Layla regained control of her voice and body. I will never forget the first time she walked on her own through our kitchen. "I'm doing it!" she exclaimed. "Let's go ice skating!" That was Layla. She could turn a small step into a giant leap, never wanting to slow down. She had months to make up for and was ready to get after it.

We spent sixteen weeks going to and from the hospital for chemotherapy, followed by another thirty days of radiation treatment. There were hard days for Layla, but for the most part, she took it all in stride. She charmed the pants off of every nurse and doctor she met, and because she ate pancakes for breakfast every morning after treatment, earned the nickname "Layla Cakes" from her Radiology nurse. The hospital became our second home and the medical staff our second family. Even now, there are days I long for that god-awful coffee and watching *Inside Out* while snuggled up with Layla in her hospital bed.

We were all so relieved to put those six months behind us. We celebrated the end of radiation with a big party, complete with face painting and a bounce house. Our brave girl had beat the hell out of cancer!

On May 31, we had a routine MRI before starting a maintenance chemo protocol at home. Once again, our world was turned upside down when we discovered that Layla had new tumor growth in both her brain and spine. Instead of starting the "easy part," we were thrust back into making decisions about treatment once again. With each new protocol we were hopeful, but nothing seemed to be able to stop the cancer's spread.

Throughout that summer our family focused on doing fun things. We spent a week on Galveston Island playing in the sand and collecting sea shells. Layla loved keeping mason jars full of them throughout our house. My favorite activity was having breakfast picnics on the porch. Layla was an early riser and would come bounding down the stairs by 6:30 a.m. Bryan and I would get our coffee while Layla spread out a blanket and gathered a pretend breakfast to serve us. Sometimes she'd invite her stuffed animals to join in. There were always lots of laughs and silly jokes.

That summer we also got another shock when we found out we were (very unexpectedly) expecting a third child. "Really God?" is what

I asked the moment I saw the positive reading on the test. What in the actual heck did God think He was doing by giving us a baby in the middle of all this? But I'll save that for another chapter.

By the third post-relapse scan in September our oncologist uttered a phrase that really brought the hammer down. "If there are things you want to do as a family, you need to do them now," he said. It was a hard suggestion to take in, but we could see the urgency on his face.

We moved our Make-A-Wish trip to Disney up by two months and left for Orlando at the end of September, just a week after Layla's fifth birthday. Physically, she was still doing well, and we had a truly magical week at Disney World. We visited the princesses (Sophia was Layla's favorite), we rode the Teacups together, and sang our hearts out with the Frozen sing-a-long. There were also days we swam and fished and took long naps. I couldn't imagine a better time together making memories as a family.

The day we packed up to come home, Layla began complaining of a severe headache. For a few hours we tried to rationalize what might be causing it, thinking it could just be a week of too much fun, not enough sleep, and poor food choices (and that was just the adults!). Quickly though, we realized this was something more serious, and we found ourselves at the children's hospital in Orlando where we were admitted to the ICU.

Layla suffered two seizures in the emergency room, which was not something we had experienced before. It was a terrifying three days, but finally we were able to be medically transported back to Dallas. Home. Sadly, an MRI showed the cancer had spread through her brain even further, reaching her cerebellum and brain stem. The medical trial we had planned to start after our vacation was now off the table. There were no more good options for Layla.

We took on a hospice care team and tried to maintain as much of a normal life for Layla as we could. Unfortunately, things progressed quickly, and we finally began to see the physical effects of the disease take a toll. Layla began losing motor function and was unable to walk or feed herself. Eventually, speaking became harder and she slept for most of the day.

On November 11, 2017, our sweet girl took her last breath and joined her Heavenly Father in her forever home. Twelve weeks later her baby sister, Evelyn Jo Rose, was born.

Our hearts are broken without Layla's sweet smile and spunky spirit, but we know that we will see her again one day.

I know our story is difficult to digest, especially for parents, but the saddest part is that it is not unique. We know dozens of children who have gone home to Jesus due to the same disease and dozens more because of various other cancers.

Although this is our story and it will be mentioned throughout, that's not what this book is about. This book is about the choice we have when life really hits the fan. It has been my experience that people either run towards God or away from Him.

Life is not a contest. My experiences are not the same as yours, but it doesn't make either of ours less significant or important. If we start measuring each other's journeys, someone's get discounted. Death, divorce, the loss of a job . . . these are only a few of the life events that can leave us questioning our faith. And there are many words you may feel like screaming when your heart is breaking and the world seems out of your control. (Newsflash: it's always out of your control.) I would never judge anyone for using those words in times of loss because Lord knows I've used them all.

But there is only one "F" word that has real power in a time of crisis. Faith. It's the word that can move mountains, close the mouths of lions, and slay giants. Hebrews 11:1 tells us that faith is "The substance of things hoped for and the evidence of things not seen." Faith is also what defends us from the never-ending attacks of the enemy around us. Ephesians 6:16 reminds us to take up the shield of faith to quench the fiery darts of the wicked one.

Without faith, I would have been stranded on an island of fear and left there for all eternity. Faith is how I get up each morning and start my day (well, that and coffee . . . all the coffee). My story, Layla's story, our family's story is far from over. God is not done with us yet and He's not done with you either.

"Faith doesn't mean you're going to get the result you want."

Chapter 1

Faith Is Easy

I have this friend named Kelly and she's hilarious. I wish I had half the humor and wit that she does. I've known Kelly for more than twenty years, but have really only *known* her for about four. We went to high school together, we were both cheerleaders—but she was two years older than me (and frankly she scared me a little). It wasn't until 2014, when we both launched businesses with the same network marketing company, that we reconnected and I realized how totally awesome she is.

We were both working moms with one-year-olds and were both desperately trying to get out of the rat race to spend more time with our babies. Although we lived several hours apart, we chatted online often and got to know one another better.

One thing I knew about my friend is that she struggled with her faith. She lost her father unexpectedly in a tragic accident when she was in her early twenties, and it rocked her belief to the core. That accident made her doubt God's goodness, and like all of us who experience loss and traumatic events in our lives, she couldn't grasp why God let that happen to her family. She was done with Him.

No judgement from me there. At that time, I had never experienced what she had.

Faith wasn't a subject we talked about much, but something hovering in the background from time to time. Not quite an elephant in the room—more of a mouse in the corner. Frankly, I didn't think I knew many people who weren't church-going Christians. At least, that was my perception. I couldn't have been more wrong.

What I didn't realize at the time is that Kelly and I were more similar in our faith than I thought. Instead of a faith in Jesus Christ, though, we were both worshipping the god of control. We were the do-it-all-ourselves, don't-need-help-from-anybody kind of women and moms. We had careers and families and we got shit done. Anyone who whined or complained was simply in our way and needed to move over. We were working-mommy soul mates.

The thing I love most about Kelly is that she's not afraid to speak her mind. Out loud. Very loudly. I'm more of a say-sarcastic-things-in-my-head or under my breath person and her boldness intrigued me. She'll be the first to tell you that her favorite word is the "F" word (the one you're more familiar with).

When I texted her with bad news or updates about Layla, she would be the one to text back a string of expletives. Strangely, that made me feel much better than someone who replied back with "praying for you guys!" and a smiley face emoji. I knew she understood loss.

I grew up in a typical Southern Baptist home. If the church doors were open, we were there. Sunday morning, Sunday night, and Wednesday evenings. I was in church choir, participated in Bible drill (if you don't know what that is, ask a Southern Baptist friend) and was involved in the youth group. In the summer, I went to church camp and generally hung out with people just like me. My Bible roots ran deep.

But when I got to high school things changed. My parents divorced and the church was not quite as inviting as it had been in the past. Our church attendance dwindled and then completely ceased. I know my mom felt awkward being there without my dad, and who could blame her? My family had been the poster children of church involvement and then, out of the blue, their marriage ended.

When I was fourteen, my impression was that their friends were hypocritical and cruel, but now I realize no one knew how to handle the situation. Throughout my adult experiences, I've seen that the typical response when someone doesn't know what to do or say is silence. It's like encountering a bear. You don't want to turn and run because the bear will take that as an invitation to chase you, but if you stay still long enough the bear will go away on its own.

That experience had a huge impact on my opinion of "church." Not necessarily on my opinion of God, but I don't think I had much of an opinion about God to begin with. He was God. His Son came to earth to save us all so that we could experience everlasting life in Heaven. I believed what happened in between was largely up to us. I might make good decisions or bad decisions, but in the end, I knew where I would end up.

It's no wonder I made more bad decisions than good. Never ever did I ask God how to proceed. I took the guns-blazing, wrecking-ball approach to my twenties.

I made the horrible mistake of buying into a self-told lie that I needed to marry immediately after graduating from college. It didn't really matter to who, so I stayed in a relationship that was doomed from the beginning. I flatly ignored every single sign God sent me to run (not walk) the other direction. Even at the very last minute, standing at the back of the church, my dad looked at me and said, "You don't have to do this." As tears welled up in my eyes, the church doors opened. I had come this far. It was too late to turn around. Friends, let me tell you that it is never too late to turn around and you should always listen to your daddy. Please learn from my mistakes.

Although I felt like I had learned much from that period of my life, I still insisted on holding onto the things I wanted too tightly. After a failed marriage, I spent the next four years chasing a boy from one side of the country to the next. Again, I ignored any prompting from the Holy Spirit that my choice was not in line with what God wanted for me. Hindsight is always 20/20 though, right? None of these decisions were necessarily conscious attempts to ignore God. I knew what I wanted (or so I thought), and would not be deterred easily from that decision. Did I mention I am stubborn and a bit of a control freak?

I realize those details might be a bit of an overshare, but I couldn't write a book about faith and leave you with the illusion that I have always lived my life with a focus on faith and trusting God. Clearly, I am still new at this.

And so, I came to God with a whole lot of baggage that morning in October 2016, when Layla was diagnosed with brain cancer. It wasn't anything He wasn't aware of or couldn't relieve me of, but I had packed for the long haul—planning to conquer the world on my own. Maybe you can relate.

The key, I found, to handing over all that baggage and the quest for control in our lives is faith. And faith is easy, right? I mean, just have some faith and life will be just peachy. Pull out that faith, sprinkle it like fairy dust, and you won't have a care in the world. Easy-peasy-lemon-squeezy, as Layla would always say.

In high school, I used to go on student council retreats to a camp with one of those ropes courses. You know, the ones that are high up in the trees, require a harness and helmet, and a release from your parents stating they're ok if you come home with fifty broken bones? I loved everything about those trips, except actually participating in the "team building," because I was (and still am) a control freak. I do not like heights—at all—and no one looks good in those harnesses. (I mean it, nobody does!)

At some point during the retreat, each of us took a turn climbing onto a platform that was probably only six feet off the ground. In my memory, however, it was closer to sixty feet. Then, we had to turn around so our backs faced the rest of the group, cross our arms, and fall backward, praying that the other twenty kids liked you enough to catch you. If your new boyfriend's ex-girlfriend was down there, forget it. Your chances were slim.

Why is it so difficult to close our eyes and let ourselves fall? Well, in high school, the answer is obvious. There are twenty hormonal, sleep-deprived maniacs (I mean teenagers) responsible for catching you. Hard pass—no thank you.

The truth is, for many of us, letting go and taking that proverbial fall into the unknown is more frightening than falling six feet into the arms of your classmates. When I'm in a situation that requires faith in someone else, these are some of the thoughts that cross my mind: there's no way they'll do this right (code for "do it the way I would do it"); and I'll just end up having to do it myself anyway. It's easier to have faith in my own ability to handle things than to leave it up to someone else who can't meet my impossible standards.

People let us down. Friends bail when we need them. Spouses forget anniversaries and co-workers will take credit for something you did. It's easier to just do all the things yourself—then no one is disappointed. No one meaning YOU. And life goes on this way until God throws you a curve ball and you are literally left with no other option; all you have is faith.

But faith is easy, right? We already established that. Just turn on that 'ol Faith Switch and watch the miracles happen. Ohhhhh . . . you don't have one of those? Faith is one of those words we throw around a whole bunch on social media. Another favorite of mine is "blessed." It sounds pretty and makes for cute Pinterest quotes and #momlife T-shirts, but rarely has any sort of real substance behind it. We treat it as a buzzword or a slogan. But what is faith really?

Faith isn't a wish. Faith is standing up in front of the enemy and refusing to let it overcome you. Faith doesn't mean you're going to get the result you want. It's accepting that Christ has a plan for everything. Notice that I didn't say "reason." I said he has a *plan* and most of the time it's impossible to see that plan through our struggle because the struggle makes everything blurry. The answer might be two feet in front of us, but we can't see anything through the blood, sweat, and tears. What could possibly be good or "planned" about watching your child lose the fight against cancer? Not a whole lot by worldly standards. I've had to accept the fact that the answer may not be something I understand until I have the chance to ask the Heavenly Father myself.

One of the first times I was truly smacked in the face by God's awesome ability to wrap us in his arms was one afternoon in the hospital. This was just after Layla's initial diagnosis and tumor removal. She was doing well after surgery and we had moved out of the ICU sooner than we expected. Praise the Lord because we finally had our own bathroom and not a shared one! The next morning the neurologist came in to give us good news. Layla was doing well enough that they were turning off the external drain that was helping regulate the pressure in her brain.

I'll pause for a second to drop some brain knowledge on you real quick. Inside our brains is fluid that continuously flows around, carrying nutrients and removing waste products from the brain. It also serves as a shock absorber for the central nervous system in case of trauma. I like to think of it as a little lazy river. If there's something blocking that river, like a tumor, the pressure of the fluid can build up and cause headaches, dizziness, and nausea. Once the tumor is removed, the body should be able to get the river moving again, but often it takes time, so a neurosurgeon will put in a temporary device that helps regulate the flow. Consider yourself a brain surgeon now. Back to where we were . . ..

About twelve hours later, an impending sense of doom washed over me. Layla was lethargic and not very responsive. I kept trying to tell the physician's assistant that something was about to happen, but I'm pretty sure he thought I was crazy. Within fifteen minutes of speaking to him, Layla's oxygen levels tanked and her blood pressure dropped dangerously low. Once she was stabilized again, we moved back to the ICU for closer observation.

It turned out her brain was not regulating the fluid the way it should with the temporary drain turned off, and we needed a backup plan. The doctors wanted to take a wait-and-see approach, but if that didn't work, we would have to put in a permanent shunt.

Similar to the temporary drain, a shunt automatically adjusts the amount of cerebral fluid in the brain when the body can't do it on its own. However, it would be inserted into Layla's skull and empty into her abdomen forever. I'll be honest, that scared the bajeezus out of me. I had no idea what that would look like for my child—not only physically, but emotionally. How would it impact her ability to do kid stuff? I remember my friend Lisa, whose child had the same type of tumor as Layla, telling me that her husband only wanted to know if his son would be able to play hockey if he had a shunt. As parents, we're always thinking about the future for our kids.

I worried over all of this for hours. I needed peace about what was happening, but couldn't find it anywhere. The next day, while our nurse was at lunch, the nurse from the room next door poked his head in to check on us. He saw Layla was having her cerebral fluid monitored and asked what happened to her. We explained she'd had a tumor removed and her body wasn't adjusting well on its own. He said, "Oh, I have a permanent one of those." What?!?!

He went on to tell us that he was "born awesome" and had always needed a shunt. I broke down in tears and felt such a weight lifted. In that moment, God knew exactly what I needed and He sent that man to our room to show us that everything would be ok. It was at that moment I knew I had a choice to make. I could let the worry and sorrow bury me, or I could take every moment and ask, "Ok God. What's the plan here?"

I promise He'll answer if you allow yourself to listen and fall back into His arms. He will always be there to catch you. And you don't have to wear that terrible ropes course harness either.

With her permission, I want to share a portion of a blog post my friend Kelly wrote shortly after Layla passed away. It sums up what many of us feel, but never say out loud. You can read the entire thing at Half-a-Hippie blog (http://halfahippie.blogspot.com/2018/03/), but this is my favorite part:

There are some things about faith that just don't work for me. It seems absurd that entire populations of people are worshipping ONE guy. Just a guy. If droves of people were worshiping a current day dude, we'd call them crazy. Praise Tom! Oh wait, that HAS happened and we DO call them crazy. So why is Christianity, or any other religion for that matter, any different? Because it's old? Because otherwise sane, smart people are believers? For me, being a true believer in the spiritual unknown and science/common sense haven't been able to live on the same street. The common sense, practical, literal part of my brain lived on one street. And the faith part of my brain was in an entirely different zip code. Sometimes I'd visit my faith that was living over in that other zip code, but always end up back at my comfy, analytical home where I'd watch those faithful people from afar. Until now, it's been one or the other for me. I was either all in on faith and God and church and religion or I was out.

But Layla.

Some of the stuff in the Bible is downright absurd. You believers must admit that it can sound bananas. But in the most unexpected place I recently found some clarity on this topic. The TV show Grey's Anatomy, of all places, had an episode called "Personal Jesus" a few weeks ago where a doctor (known as the super religious, Jesus loving doc) experiences several challenges to her faith in one day. In one scene, she is talking with a patient that has landed himself in the hospital because he has taken to hurting/punishing himself based on his very literal translation of the bible. She tells him the Bible is full of stories and metaphors and things aren't meant to be taken so literally, that it is meant to be followed "within reason." Ding, ding, ding. I can get on board with this.

For a long time, I wasn't all that sure about heaven. This goes hand in hand with my faith struggle I suppose. I mean if the dude ain't real, then surely his home in the clouds is a crock too, right? Could this be another example of a bible story taken too literally?

But Layla.

When you pray and pray and beg and beg and hope and hope and just KNOW that your friend with faith the size of the universe will have things swing her way and that God will save her baby, and then her baby isn't saved, your already fragile faith can really take a hit. Why would I . . . why should I, believe in that guy?

Because Layla.

You see, I just can't live in a world where my friend never sees her baby again. That world just can't exist. It can't. My heart can't handle that. My head can't either. I simply MUST believe that she's in heaven, whatever that may be . . . whatever form it may take, waiting on her family. And it's not sad for her, she's not lonely there, all pitifully waiting like a lost child. She's good. She's well. She's whole. She is where cancer can no longer rob her of her spunk and brilliance and sweet, squeaky little voice. And her mom and dad and brother and new baby sister will see her again. I HAVE to believe this. I realize the doubters (and I include myself in that bunch) will say I'm just making this whole thing fit my current needs and address my current heartbreak. I don't know. Maybe that's true. I'm fine with that. I've made peace with that.

Because Layla.

One little girl has changed me at my core. Moved me so deeply that I'll never be the same. So much so that I'm taking faith lessons not only from her, but from stupid TV shows too. But hey, you take the lessons where you get them right?

You see I have friends that I respect very much on both sides of the faith fence. The non-believers appeal to my common-sense core, my science mind, the doubter. But the believers appeal to my heart. And in this case, the heart wins.

Because Layla.

Kelly's words bring tears to my eyes each time I read them. Mostly because it's a beautiful thing to know your child had that kind of profound impact on another person, but also because her thoughts have been my thoughts. In my darkest moments alone with God, I could feel myself questioning what I was doing there on my knees. Why wasn't He healing her? The God I knew was fully capable, so why wouldn't He just do it? It's an answer I still don't have and may never get until I ask Him face-to-face. Still, I know that He is always good, even though it doesn't always feel good to my aching heart.

"Don't miss out on something spectacular because you're convinced you can't do it yourself."

Chapter 2

Letting Go of Control

Becoming a parent has mellowed me out to some extent. When Layla was born, I began to realize just how much was not within my control—things like diaper blow outs and feeding schedules. But the desire to control everything was still sitting right under the surface. It just manifested itself in different ways. For example: having the dishwasher loaded properly, folding towels the correct way, and being on time. (My motto has always been, "If you're not early, you're late.")

I guess, technically, all those things are still within my control as long as I'm willing to do the work myself. You can't ask for help and then tell the helper they're doing it wrong. Trust me on this, they don't appreciate it and the offers of help quickly disappear.

My overinflated sense of control can easily be compared to that of my dog's. Her name is Babe and I often refer to her as the best worst dog you'll ever find. A few months after Bryan and I got married, we decided to try fostering a dog. We already had a dog, but for some reason I thought adding one more to the mix was a good idea.

This is often the trend for newlyweds it seems: marriage, house, dog, baby. Who were we to mess with the correct procedure?

I had been volunteering with a local rescue organization for several months and I actually had a different dog in mind. However, the rescue organization had an urgent need to find a foster home for a dog recovering from surgery. Poor Babe had been kicked by a horse and suffered a severe broken leg. So into our home she came. Part of our job was to keep her calm (ha!) and help with her physical therapy.

Trying to keep a one-year-old dog from getting into everything is much like doing the same for a one-year-old child. Add to that the fact that she is a fifty-pound Pitbull/Tasmanian devil mix. Eventually she recovered enough to visit the homes of other people interested in adopting her, but there was just one problem—my husband. He had fallen in love with Babe and had a hard time finding any other home "acceptable." Long story short, Babe has been with us for over eight years now.

Once I realized this dog was staying with us, I decided to take her to obedience training (otherwise known as a waste of my money). It wasn't a waste because the training was poor, but the trainers (me and Bryan) did not reinforce her behavior the way we should have at home.

One of the first things we worked on was teaching Babe to wait before barging through a door. It is more than just good manners, it was supposed to show her that she wasn't in charge. She must wait for the master to *allow* her to enter (or exit). In case you're wondering, she routinely barrels over anyone and everyone as she forces her way out the door first. Like I said, money well spent. She also barks at anything that moves outside, jumps on people, and generally thinks of our furniture as her domain.

She does have some redeeming qualities. She's a great snuggler and has the scariest bark on the block. Just ask anyone who has mistakenly let themselves into our backyard without being invited. Best worst dog ever.

How often are we the ones barreling out the door first? We're ready to take on the day and the rest of the world before anyone else has the chance. But more often than not, we end up tripping over ourselves and knocking everyone else over. In my head, God spends most of His day looking at me and just shaking His head—much the same way I shake my head at the dog when she seems confused about having to get off the couch. "If you'd only listen!" we both say.

So how do I cope when so much of life seems to overwhelm me? There's real merit to the saying "when it rains, it pours." I've often raised my eyes to the sky and said, "Geez God, can we catch a break?"

That's pretty much how I felt when, in the midst of Layla's relapse, I discovered I was pregnant. I woke up one morning and coffee sounded gross. Immediately I knew something was not right. Me and coffee are buddies. I would never treat coffee that way! My instincts stepped in and my brain said, "You're pregnant!" NOOOOOOOO. This couldn't be possible, could it? It only took two minutes for that snarky pregnancy test to tell me yes-this-is-really-happening with its little smiley face on a stick. Just when I thought I might be gaining some control back over life, God reeled me back to reality.

We all have those moments in life when we're smacked in the face by something so big we automatically think, "I just can't do this!" Instead of actually meaning that, though, we pull out our hubris and start to take it on ourselves—sometimes with a chisel, sometimes with a sledgehammer. I prefer the sledgehammer approach, myself. It makes a mess, but it's much more satisfying. I can clean up the mess up later.

Do you use the sledgehammer on your problems, or are you more the chisel type? Slowly but surely, chipping away at your problems a little at a time, your result will likely look more like a work of art than mine will, but that's not really the point. Either way, we're both working on our own and making things happen on our time instead of God's. It's human instinct to want to control our situations when things seem over our heads, but we're making a hot mess of life on our own.

So, when life was so far over my head it was like trying to see over the Rocky Mountains on my tip-toes, I had to ask myself what other choice did I have except to place all that junk at the foot of the cross and admit I couldn't handle it? I can say from personal experience that it is miserable carrying that weight around all the time, but I always saw letting it go as a failure. If I couldn't fix a problem on my own, I had either failed to deal with life or failed to get past adversity. In truth, giving my problems to God is the *only* way to deal with it. If we're not willing to admit that we can't, we aren't allowing God to show us that He *can*. God is able to do immeasurably more than all we ask or imagine (Ephesians 3:20).

I constantly remind myself that God is able to provide beyond my wildest dreams. If you had asked me eighteen months ago what was beyond my wildest imaginings, I would have said that Layla's cancer would be gone and never return again. Now, maybe even more crazy to me, is taking our experience and doing something amazing with it. I wrote a book for goodness sake! On real paper and everything! I am not one to push myself too far outside my comfort zone for others to see, but for probably only the third time in my life, I felt a prompting and actually said "Yes."

As freeing as it is, letting go of that control freak baggage comes with its own baggage. The first thing I noticed was my ability to see everyone else's control freakishness. And you know what control freaks don't like? Being told they're a control freak.

I often have to keep myself from acting like the newly anointed Queen of Living Free. Even well-meaning comments like, "Girl, you've got to let go of that," are not as well received as I would like. I'm learning to keep my mouth shut on the subject, at least with people I value relationships with. It's not my words that are going to help someone see where they need to release control. Only the prompting of the Holy Spirit can tackle that.

Years ago, I dated a guy who introduced me to the "Circle of

Control." The concept is that there are only a few things within your immediate influence. That's what is considered "in your circle." Everything else is out of your control. It's a remarkably short list when you get down to it. Actually, your feelings and your reactions are the only things on it.

Yep, that's about it. We could get into mundane things like what you wear or where you live, but what if you're required to wear a uniform for work? That's out of your control unless you decide to go get a new job. Aside from things like that, most of life can be boiled down to two things outside your control: others' feelings and reactions.

Do you see where I'm going with this? I'm oversimplifying here, but sometimes that's the way it needs to be in order for people to grasp the concept. Not because they aren't smart enough, but because we tend to get all caught up in the details.

The reality of life is that we have little to no control over our existence, and I don't mean that in some existential crisis way. When we live our lives trying to control each detail, we are wasting energy—either because it's impossible to expect someone to do things the exact way you would want them or it's counter to what God really wants for us.

I'll give you an example of a newly married couple (no names used to protect the innocent). The wife very much wanted the husband to *want* to attend church, so she nagged him a whole bunch. When that didn't work, she sulked. But someone always ended up disappointed on Sunday mornings. Finally, she gave up. Instead of nagging she prayed. "Lord, please make my husband do what I want." Just kidding . . . she prayed that the Lord would soften her husband's heart about whatever was keeping him from attending church, and that God would speak to him about why he needed to be there.

It didn't happen overnight or with some lightning bolt, but gradually she began to see a change. One Sunday morning the husband asked, "Are we going to church this morning?" Convincing her husband to go to church was outside this young lady's circle of control, but it wasn't outside of God's.

How much time and energy have I wasted, attempting to put things in their perfect place? I tried desperately to manage situations on my own. I thought that if something was difficult, it just required more effort, like pushing a car uphill. I never stopped to consider if it was my car to push. I had no concept of stepping back and waiting patiently for God to reveal which was the right car to me. Once I was able to wait, I realized I may still have to push the car uphill, but at least I'm not pushing it alone!

> **In this world you will have trouble. But take heart! I have overcome the world.**
> **(John 16:33)**

One of my favorite ways to start my day is with Sarah Young's book, *Jesus Calling*. Each page is a short devotional, but the interesting thing about it is that no matter how many times I've started it over I never get the same message twice. The Bible's ability to speak to me at exactly the place I'm in is fascinating. Seriously, if you don't have a copy you need to pick one up. Or send me your address and I'll pay to have one sent over.

I'll let you in on a little secret about me. I'm the type of person who likes to read the end of the book first. I don't like surprises, so I want to know how the story ends or at least know what comes next. So, it should come as no surprise that one morning I was skipping ahead in my *Jesus Calling* devotional. God used my impatient tendencies to help me through something I was struggling with at the time. As I skipped ahead, I opened to a page that read, "Give up the illusion that you deserve a problem-free life."[1]

Ouch!

I think as Americans we feel entitled to a worry-free existence. I realize this is a gross generalization, but it's no coincidence that #firstworldproblems trends daily on social media. We treat it as a joke, but take a look at what comes up under that hashtag and you'll see some of the ridiculousness firsthand. Some of my favorites include, "Seriously, no wi-fi?" and "It's fifty-five degrees outside and my heated seats are broken. Brrrr."

I have no problem admitting my own contribution to this type of complaint. I've felt the overwhelming irritation at Starbucks for being out of pumpkin loaf and let the whole world know my disappointment over Facebook. The thing about a trouble-free life is that it leaves no room for faith. Our response to hardships is so much more important than God's immediate resolution of them. The response is where we are challenged to activate what we say we believe.

Nowhere in the Bible is this described more beautifully than in the book of Job. This is a book that never had much meaning to me before now. Job had it all: a beautiful family, wealth, and a deep love for God, but it all was taken from him by Satan. He lost all of his children, all of his servants, and all of his wealth in a moment. He even suffered great physical ailments that left him in incredible pain. Still, even after all that, he praised God. Even after his wife told him that he should curse God, he praised God.

"Shall we accept good from God, and not trouble?" was Job's response to his wife. That, my friends, is where the rubber meets the road for me. I cannot seek truth from God and expect only sunshine and roses, but I can honestly say I did not truly believe that until October 2016. Mostly it was because I had never faced something I so desperately needed God for, something so outside my control that my entire existence was shaken to its core.

The book of John is pretty specific that we won't have a trouble-free life, but that isn't the only place that we're told life won't be easy. The first chapter of James tells us that we should be excited when we face trouble:

> **Consider it pure joy when you face trials. The testing of your faith produces perseverance. (James 1:2-3)**

> **When you ask, you must believe and not doubt, because the one who doubts is like a wave of the sea, blown and tossed by the wind. (James 1:6)**

Really? Pure joy, huh? Yes, it was pure joy to learn that my four-year-old had brain cancer. (I feel like I need to use a sarcasm disclaimer. Maybe I should have put one at the very beginning of the book.)

It's slightly ridiculous to assume we'll feel joyful over hardships. I can't think of a time where anyone has rejoiced over losing a loved one or a divorce (ok, well maybe some people have with that one).

To me, this verse only appeals to two sets of people. The first group are those who have never known real hardship. It's something they would quote (well meaning, of course) to a friend going through a difficult time. People say stupid stuff. I could write an entire chapter on just that. The second group are those who have walked through hell and come out a different person.

It's basically the Bible verse where we get, "If it doesn't kill you, it makes you stronger." Which is another thing stupid—I mean, well-meaning—people say.

Are you in one of those two groups of people? Maybe you're the well-meaning friend who has said some really stupid stuff. I apologize that I keep calling you stupid, but you are. It's ok, we forgive you. We understand you have no real clue and only want to help. I can promise you that a friend who says stupid things is better to have than a friend who says nothing at all. Again, that could be an entire chapter on its own.

So how do we wrap our heads around finding joy in times where life feels out of control? Honestly, it's not something that's possible without knowing the true presence of the Holy Spirit in our lives. We cannot do it without accepting that He is with us always. We cannot do it without believing that He is the light in the darkest of spaces. We most certainly cannot do it without knowing He is the friend who sits with us in the hard places, never passing judgement or attempting to be a fixer. Again, leave it to the lovely Sarah Young in *Jesus Calling* to explain God's promises with the words I don't have:

> Most Christians accept this teaching as truth but ignore it in their daily living. Some ill-taught or wounded believers fear (and may even resent) My awareness of all they do, say and think. A few people center their lives around this glorious promise and find themselves blessed beyond all expectations. When My Presence is the focal point of your consciousness, all the pieces of your life fall into place. As you gaze at Me through the eyes of your heart, you can see the world around you from My perspective. The fact that *I am with you* makes every moment of your life meaningful.[2]

There are days when I look in the mirror and I don't recognize the person I see, and it's more than just the extra gray hair and wrinkles that come with being closer to forty than I'd like to admit. I see a woman who let go of her need to have everything come out exactly her way.

Habits are hard to break, though, and those urges creep back into my behavior from time to time. That's because letting go of control isn't an easy feat. Please know that I'm still a work in progress, just like you, but mighty things happen when we begin practicing the discipline of allowing God to be in charge. One of my favorite quotes from A.W. Tozer is:

> God is looking for people through whom He can do the impossible. What a pity we plan to do only the things that we can do by ourselves.[3]

Don't miss out on something spectacular because you're convinced you can't do it yourself.

"Faith fills the gap between what we want and what God has planned."

Chapter 3

When Prayer Expectations Don't Meet Our Reality

Prayer was not a foreign concept to me as a child or young adult. As I mentioned, I grew up "in the church," so I knew what it was to pray. As a kid, I prayed for toys I wanted or a snow day from school. Which, let me tell you, was a tall order growing up in North Dallas. The most we ever get are ice days, and because no one knows how to drive when it rains, let alone ices up, the city basically shuts down. Ice is not as much fun as snow because there's nothing to actually play with and you're stranded indoors.

That's another thing about cold weather in Dallas and the South in general. We are completely unprepared when it comes to dressing for temperatures below fifty degrees. Parents put socks on their kids' hands and they wear rain boots instead of snow boots. I'm guilty of both things.

But, where was I? Ah yes, prayer. Bow head, fold hands, let your mind wander until the preacher says "Amen." Try not to fall asleep. I think that about sums up prayer for many of us.

But what about when you really *need* something? I'm not talking about wanting a raise so you can buy a fancier house or getting an acceptance letter to college, but a *real* need. Like when your marriage needs a serious intervention because you and your spouse are sleeping in separate rooms, or you need a job because you're about to be evicted and living on the street. Or, in our case, our child needs a miracle because she has brain cancer. I think all those things qualify as pretty hefty needs to pray for.

Is there a specific way we need to pray to have our prayers answered? If our situation doesn't improve, does that mean we did it wrong? Did God not hear us? Did He determine we weren't worthy of His miracle?

I wrestled with all these questions over a thirteen-month period. Like, heavily wrestled. Me and God, toe-to-toe, in my closet, fists raised, many choice words uttered. How can you God? Why won't you God? This isn't fair. Take me, not her.

God doesn't mind the wrestling. In fact, in Genesis 32 there is an actual, physical wrestling match between Jacob and an angel. Jacob was at the precipice of his faith journey, and that wrestling match is significant because Jacob was renamed at its finish. His renaming was a symbol of his growing faith and overcoming many adversities.

In case you're not familiar with Jacob's story in the Bible, he wasn't exactly the greatest guy around. He tricked his dying father into granting him his brother's birthright and then ran away like a coward. The most confusing part of the story for me is when God reveals himself to Jacob in a dream and promises to bless him and never leave him. Excuse me, what?

Do you ever feel like saying that to God? Maybe you know a Jacob in your life. Someone who isn't a very good person, yet seems to be always have things go their way? I can't answer on God's behalf as to what is going on with our Jacobs, but I do know that dream was a turning point for the Jacob of the Old Testament. As we grow in our faith, we transform through God's grace.

My son Daniel has a book that he loves to have Bryan and me read to him. It's called *Far Flutterby*[4]. It's about a little caterpillar named Cody who longs for so much more in his life than he already has. All the other caterpillars are content with eating and sleeping all day long, but not Cody. Then he meets a beautiful bird and colorful butterfly, who both promise him that God has great things in store for him. Cody finds this hard to believe. How can God use a lowly caterpillar?

One day, he has the urge to wrap himself in a cocoon and, hanging there, he waits and waits. He waits so long that he becomes increasingly frustrated. He struggles and wriggles in the cocoon until he's sweaty and tired. Right as he starts to lose hope, he breaks free—and realizes he now has beautiful wings.

The struggle and waiting for the blessing is the hardest part. If you're the slightest bit impatient (like me), it seems like hell on earth to wait. Little by little, we will eventually begin to see God revealing his great promises to us. Masterpieces take time to create.

Even hiding in the closet, railing at God with all my tears, I could feel the presence of the Holy Spirit comforting me. I wish I had the exact words to describe what that feels like, but for me, it was an overwhelming sense of calm after the rage. I hated what we were going through, but always felt like it would be ok in the end. There must be a reason for all of this and even in those last few days I would tell people, "I just know that she's going to wake up tomorrow and walk down those stairs."

She may not have walked into my arms again, but she did walk into the arms of her Savior. He welcomed her to Heaven, completely healed and whole once again. Before Layla passed away, I read the story of Lazarus over and over again, convinced that our story would end the same way. The New Testament is filled with the kind of miracles I hoped for daily and I know God is capable of providing them. Our miracle simply didn't turn out the way I wanted.

I'll admit, I'm scarred all over from the experience, but those scars are proof that I've been to battle and lived through it. I wanted to turn away from God more times than I care to admit. It's difficult to keep letting life beat you down when Satan is whispering in your ear. It's the reason I've never understood the sport of boxing. Why would someone willingly let themselves be punched in the face? I get that the point is *not* to get hit, but it's somewhat inevitable. Even great boxers like Muhammad Ali leave the ring with black eyes and broken noses.

The place where we're ready to give up is the place where we have to stand our ground. I continued to ask God for answers to my questions, even if they didn't come in the form I hoped for, or even at all.

My prayer efforts were matched and exceeded by the thousands of people who were praying for us across the country—maybe even across the globe. Social media can be an amazing thing when it comes to crisis.

When Layla passed away, my inbox was flooded by messages from strangers who were deeply impacted by our loss. Although we didn't know one another, we were all left with many, many questions. Together, we experienced the disconnect between what we prayed for and how the story ended. There were so many hearts left questioning why our healing miracle never came through.

Prayer is a funny thing, you see. God is not a genie that grants wishes when you find Him. Now, I don't know about you, but I grew up with some of the best Disney movies, like *The Lion King* and *Aladdin*. I loved Robin Williams as the genie, although I didn't get most of the jokes until I was older. It's easy to imagine what kinds of things we'd ask a genie for, should we come across a magic lamp. Many of us have that same image of God in our head. Ask and ye shall receive, right?

What image do you see in your head as you pray? Do you imagine God sitting on his throne like Joaquin Phoenix in *Gladiator*, peering down at us and giving a thumbs up or thumbs down to our prayers? Do you believe your answer depends on his mood that day? Are we being judged on the content and grammar of our prayer? Did we use the right words at the right time of day with no distractions? Do you believe your past sins get in the way of your current situation and His ability and desire to show you favor?

Friends, our God is awesome. He is not wishy-washy, nor does He allow a bad day to make decisions for Him. He was not looking down at the thousands of people praying for Layla, trying to determine if we were worthy. He wasn't in a bad mood the day she relapsed or the day she took her last breath. He knew the exact number of seconds she would have on earth and the impact she would make. His plan has been set in place since the beginning of time.

Then what's the point of praying, you ask? An excellent and complex question that I believe we've all had at some point in our lives. I have struggled with this on multiple occasions and have come to the following conclusion: it's a matter of faith. Oh, the old F-word again. Yes, I know that's a bit frustrating when you want a real, concrete answer.

The truth of the matter is that smarter people than me have tried to answer this question for centuries. I bet that for every article you find in a Google search (because, yes, I Googled it), you will get a different answer. It seems to me there is no right and perfect answer because we are not God. We cannot possibly know His thoughts or conceive of His intentions, but we have our Bibles as a guide. We know the Bible teaches that God has a predetermined plan, but it also teaches us about the importance of prayer. Even if we cannot wrap our heads around it, we have to believe that both aspects of Christianity are true. Again, that's where faith comes in.

As I already mentioned, prayers are not wishes although most of us treat them that way. We ask for material possessions and immediate responses, things to make our lives more comfortable. What we're missing is the ability to see God work BIG.

What does it mean to see God work big in our lives? Curing cancer would have been a pretty big answer to prayer for me, that's for sure. What I noticed, during those months of begging for a miracle, was that I began praying for more than just that. I prayed that God would use Layla's life and my life as a way to point people towards God, and that our experience would bring transformation to the thousands of people praying with me. I had no idea what that would look like, and frankly, I often feel like the least equipped person to be speaking to others on the topic. I have zero background in theology or biblical studies, but God knew what was coming and He has given me the words that each person reading this book needs to hear. Somehow, He brings it all together, and Layla's life will continue to shine far beyond the 1,877 days she lived here on earth.

Another important tenet of prayer is that it draws us closer to Him. When we humbly come before God with our requests, we show Him that we cannot do life without Him. His true desire is that we have a relationship with Him, and when we lean on Him for both the big and small things we draw closer to Him. Each time we deepen that dependence and relationship, it becomes easier to let go of control.

If we refuse to let go, we can still end up where we need to be, but I guarantee the process will be harder, with more speed bumps and potholes along the way. It's like getting to a fork in the road and trying to decide which way to go. God may be prompting you to go the right direction, but you are hell-bent on doing it your way, so off you go. I hope you brought a few spare tires because you're going to need them.

That's not to say that when you listen to God and go the way He asks that it will be smooth sailing. We will still encounter hardships and obstacles that can derail us because that's part of life. Keeping our eyes fixed on the Father is how we navigate around those obstacles. Each step on the rocky terrain will "supply what is lacking in your faith." (1 Thessalonians 3:10)

The enemy will always attempt to make our walk with God difficult and cumbersome. We must be vigilant to stay on course because those obstacles are meant to steer us in the wrong direction. Are there times that we *need* to fall into the potholes of life? Absolutely. Those potholes give us the opportunity to reach up and ask for the help we need to get out. Faith assures us that we're not doing life alone and that our rescue will come.

I've always found 1 John 5:14 to be an interesting verse. It says, "This is the confidence that we have in Him, that, if we ask anything according to His will, He heareth us."

Oh, how I wish I could change that verse to say, "If we ask anything according to His will, He makes it so."

God hears us. He always does, but that doesn't mean we are guaranteed to have the outcome we want. That's where faith steps in. Faith fills the gap between what WE want and what God has planned. He did not will bad things to happen to you or me, but He will always allow for a beautiful answer in its place, something so unexpected and amazing that only God could have designed it. Sometimes we have to wait for it (and it's the waiting that kills me), but that's faith.

One of my favorite quotes from Dr. Tony Evans is, "Faith is acting like it is so, even when it is not so, so that it might be so, simply because God said so." I take that as a roundabout way of saying God has plans for me (He said so), so I will live as if it's true (acting like it is so), until the day it is (so that it might be so).

Faith can move a mountain. That's what the Bible tells us in Matthew 17:20 (and in the books of Mark and Luke). But what if it's not the exact mountain you wanted moved? How frustrating it is to stand in front of a mountain, with all the faith you have mustered up, and the mountain next to you moves instead.

I experienced this countless times. After each MRI Layla had and being told her cancer was still spreading, I found myself on the floor of my closet, fists in the air, yelling "WTF Lord! I have faith as big as a boulder and still my mountain won't move!" (I warned y'all there were many choice words screamed in the closet.) What then? Do we throw faith out the window because the magic words didn't work? The late pastor Chuck Smith said, "The greatest faith is not manifested in my escaping suffering, but to trust the keeping of myself to the will and purpose of God if it should call for suffering."[5]

That's pretty heavy. My faith isn't tied to His ability to improve circumstances, but to continue in His work when He doesn't. Especially when He doesn't. A lack of faith did not cause me to lose my daughter, but its existence does require me to continue to accept and trust in His good works.

Has your faith been tied to a request that has gone unanswered? An unmoved mountain? What effect has that had on your relationship with God? For most people, and reasonably so, this results in a falling out with God.

I will not hesitate to admit that I am only human, and there are days when I look at kids winning their battle against cancer and think, "Why them?" It's almost against human nature to take delight in another's victory when our own losses are so great. But another child's life was not swapped out for Layla's. She did not die so they could survive. So I allow myself to feel joy that another family was spared the life-altering sadness that comes with losing a child.

I've learned that payer and faith are disciplined activities. Just like I can't expect to step into a gym once and exit with washboard abs, I cannot expect my Heavenly Father to make me feel all the warm fuzzies because I bow my head once. We live in a world of pain and suffering. It sounds cliché, but it's the truth. I've seen people have visceral reactions to that comment before.

People who are struggling with faith see it as the Christian scapegoat. Those crazy Bible beaters have an excuse for everything, they say. Answered prayers and God gets all the glory. Unanswered prayers and it's not His fault. I'm sorry to say that I don't have anything different to provide on the topic or some way to convince them otherwise.

Like it or not, bad stuff happens to good people. Not because God doesn't care or love us, but because the enemy (that's Satan y'all) is an ever-present force that we have to guard ourselves against. When we finally realize that faith gives us strength, we become much less vulnerable to Satan's tricks. He still comes at us, though. Even more so than before because now you're a challenge. He's like the creepy guy at the bar who thinks you're playing hard to get because you won't give him your number. No dude . . . she's just not that into you.

Someone who has lost hope, believes in nothing, and is willing to take Satan's lashes is an easy target; but woah, a person who still believes God is good in the hardest of circumstances is going to give ol' Satan a run for his money. To quote Beth Moore in her Bible study, *The Quest,* "For us to persevere or dare to grow in our love for God while we momentarily do not love His observable way is no small wound on the devil's brow."[6] Or as I like to say, not quite as eloquently as Beth, "Please give it up, Satan . . . you're just embarrassing yourself at this point."

Thus, he tries harder and gets craftier. Recognizing him for what he is allows us to keep him out. He comes wielding fear and doubt and anger and bitterness, looking for the smallest opening to give him a foothold. The more we exercise our prayer and faith, the stronger we become against him. Hebrews tells us to "continually offer to God a sacrifice of praise." In *Jesus Calling,* author Sarah Young extends this to also include the sacrifice of time:

Let my love enfold you in the radiance of My Glory. Sit still in the Light of My Presence, and receive My Peace. These quiet moments with Me transcend time, accomplishing far more than you can imagine. Bring Me the sacrifice of your time, and watch to see how abundantly I bless you and your loved ones.[7]

I'll give you an example. When I decided to write "31 Days of Faith" as an Instagram series in January of 2018, I knew it would be an exercise in discipline. Each day I committed to exploring a new aspect of faith, reading the Bible, and then putting it out into the webisphere. I prayed that someone else would see it and it would resonate with them.

From the very first day I posted, it didn't take long for some yucky feelings to creep their way into my heart. I began to feel angry and deeply sad. Some might say that those feelings are a normal part of the grieving cycle, which they are, but with each positive comment on my blog or Facebook page or every uplifting message I received, I found myself doubting what I was doing and my abilities. Clearly people were responding positively, but Satan hated my work more than an internet troll. What I was saying was having a profound impact on others and making his work harder. He needed me to feel terrible. Being able to recognize his tricks is what saved me in the end. Satan isn't all that original in his ways. He's easy to spot if you know what to look for.

Priscilla Shirer is one of my favorite authors and she writes amazing Bible studies, including *Armor of God*. This book is where she exposes the devil's playbook. She helps bring light to all his tactics and the weapons we all possess to fend him off. At one point, she asks the reader to write down the people or circumstances they are currently wrestling with. She then goes on to say, "Whatever you've written above, whether a person or circumstance, it is not your real problem. Hear that again: *IT is NOT your REAL problem.*" And then, further down, I have highlighted, "Everything that occurs in the visible, physical world is directly connected to the wrestling match being waged in the invisible, spiritual world."[8]

For me, this was a truly eye-opening lesson. My control and my perceived handle on the situation had nothing to do with me at all. Satan was the mastermind behind the doubts I was experiencing. He's an excellent magician whose entire goal is to distract you with what you can see with your own two eyes. When we let go of our need for control, it allows us to see the world through the eyes of the Holy Spirit—a world where God's desires and will for our lives is fantastically greater than what we can imagine. I realize that's difficult to digest when your life has hit the skids. Stick with me here. We're only on chapter three.

"When we are deep in a hole with our darkest feelings, the natural reaction is to get ourselves out."

Chapter 4

Filling the Empty Spaces

In the aftermath of loss, the quietness can be overwhelming. It's a constant reminder that something is absent . . . the absence of a beloved voice, the empty seat at the dinner table, even the bickering that occurs between siblings. That was the first transition our family had to make in those initial days. Our house had always been filled with a squeaky, Disney-princess-like voice, and suddenly it was gone. I drove Daniel to school and the car was silent. As the little brother, he was so used to being the listener that it took him weeks to realize he now had a chance to get a word in edgewise. Even as a two-year-old, he recognized the gaping hole that was present.

We limped through the holidays that first year with brave faces, but I'd be lying if I said I wasn't glad when the season was all over. New Year's Day rolled around, and we had dinner with friends and kicked off the first meeting of Layla's Legacy Foundation.

Layla's dream was to be a nurse when she grew up so she could take care of all the little kids. By focusing on raising funds for pediatric brain cancer research and providing financial support to families going through the same horrible journey we experienced, we are honoring the future she won't have.

Since things aren't official until they're posted on social media, we took a few photos of the group that had gathered. One of the parents and one of all the kids together. The light streaming in through the blinds made me think Layla was there with us all in the kitchen, smiling her silly smile next to her brother. Every photo of our family or friends feels like it has a gaping hole in it. Which begs the question: how do we fill that empty space?

The natural reaction, initially, for us was to stay busy. As long as we were moving and doing there wasn't time to think about how we actually felt. Two days after Layla's death, Bryan was building a shed in the backyard with his brother, and I was refinishing furniture in the garage with my sister. To strangers, we looked like two people who took a week off from work to get some things done around the house, but the activity kept our minds occupied.

I know for certain that when we had visitors at the house that first week, they were utterly confused. You could see the look on their faces when, instead of seeing two parents sitting on the couch in tears, they got two crazy people building stuff outdoors. Do you find yourself doing that when you're stressed? I know people who eat or drink, or maybe they bake or clean the house obsessively. It's all the same end game. We're distracting ourselves in the hope that we'll forget what is actually happening.

Eventually, it all caught up to us, and we had to face the fact that the time had come to actually address what we were trying to ignore— our grief. Grief is a tricky one because it's one thing to process your own grief, but an entirely different situation when you throw someone else's feelings into the mix.

I was somewhat prepared for this because I'd witnessed other couples lose their children. But I really began thinking more about it after a conversation with another mom who had lost her child to brain cancer.

"You know losing a child is a marriage killer," she told me. Her words hung in the air like dense fog. I'd met this person all of five minutes ago, and THIS is what she tells me? "Yes," I replied, "I've seen it happen to many couples." (Insert awkward silence.)

This conversation came at a point in our journey when it seemed unlikely that Layla was going to lose her battle, at least in our minds. She was still an active, happy kid doing all the things she loved, like coloring, playing with her toys, and bossing her little brother around. We were easily able to ignore the eventual reality.

In hindsight though, I can see that conversation was leading me to consider what those empty spaces would look like if we faced the unimaginable. Not only would Layla's loss leave a void, but there was the possibility of another if I lost my spouse, too.

One hundred and three days later, we watched our daughter's body be placed into the back of the funeral home's van. Even in the weeks leading up to her death, I quietly observed the differences in the way people grieve. I saw the way fear, anger, sadness, and denial all play a role when we're wrestling with an inevitable loss. Grief is the most raw, personal, complex human emotion we're capable of because it can manifest itself in so many different ways. Some lash out in anger. Others withdraw from life. Many mask their feelings by self-medicating. Outwardly they tell a different story, but grief is the true master of behavior.

Any loss can wreck a marriage or relationship. Losing a parent, a sibling, or even a friend can leave one partner reeling without seeming to affect the other. Even the loss of a job can be processed differently between spouses. When you're knee-deep in your own feelings, it's hard to understand why your partner doesn't appear to be as impacted the way you are. Why aren't you worried? How is it that you sleep at night while I lie awake? Anger and resentment easily builds to a point where all communication stops. You sit together in silence, both wishing the other understood how you felt. For many months, as we prayed for complete healing for our daughter, I also prayed for God to save my marriage. I prayed we would be able to recognize each other's needs and support one another through those moments. I knew in my heart that we would grieve differently and that was okay.

Unfortunately, I've watched other couples walk through child loss in the same way we have and that stranger (who is now my friend) was absolutely right. Grief is a marriage killer because it's an easy "in" for Satan—he can get a foothold in our bitterness and anger. I leaned heavily on Psalm 147:3 as a way for Bryan and I to grieve together: "He heals the broken hearted and binds up their wounds."

I came to understand that it wasn't just the two of us in mourning. God mourned our loss with us because He understands what it's like to lose a child. He allows us to see each other's pain even when it looks different from our own, to give each other space or a hug when it's needed and, most importantly, to destroy the enemy's plan before it can take up residence in those empty spaces. Although we tried, there was no distraction big enough to fill the empty space permanently. I've been told eventually it will feel different. The hole won't seem *as* big or *as* deep, but it will never be fully filled. I haven't decided whether that makes me feel better or not. In some ways that empty space is what keeps my memories fresh. If it changes, will my memories change? Will photos be the only way I'll have to remember the years she was with us?

You see, even though my journey to let go of control started with grief, I've been carrying around a hole in my life for as long as I can remember. We all are. One of the questions I've asked myself in times of reflection is how giving up control fills up those empty spaces. It seems counter-intuitive. Typically, when we think about giving something up, we imagine a space where that thing was. Like when we ripped the shower out of our bathroom—there was a gaping hole for weeks until we hired someone to redo it. (That's how many of the do-it-yourself projects go in our home. We're quick to tear it out, slow to build it back. Maybe you can relate.)

God designed us with this void intentionally, but not so we could try to fill it ourselves. He created it to spark the desire to have a deep, meaningful relationship with Him, our Heavenly Father. No one is exempt from this feeling of emptiness because we were all created by Him, and no person and no earthly thing can fill it besides Him. Without Him, we attempt to fill the emptiness however we can.

It reminds me of the shape sorter toy Daniel loved playing with when he was little. He would dump all the shape blocks out and put them in the corresponding holes, over and over again. The tricky part was when two shapes were very similar. Sometimes, this resulted in him forcing a shape through the wrong hole, because technically it "fit" with a little assistance from his fist. Then he would say "Tada!" and be super proud of his accomplishment.

Don't we all do this same thing? We see something that looks like it might fit perfectly into that void and we convince ourselves that it *must*, so we mash and mash until we're pleased with our work. Tada! Look what I did! And then we post a selfie on Instagram to make sure everyone knows about it.

Still, the hole persists, and we continue trying to fill it with all manner of vices. For some, it's the obvious: drugs, alcohol, sex, gambling, or food. For others, the addiction is less obvious. Online shopping, binge watching television, even our children can be the thing we think will fill that void. The hole feels biggest when we are furthest from God, and the manner in which we cope speaks volumes about our faith.

Beth Moore put it perfectly in *The Quest*, when she said, "Perhaps no other indicator gives a more accurate reading of our heart condition than how we console ourselves."[9]

When we are deep in a hole with our darkest feelings, the natural reaction is to get ourselves out. Instinctually, we know that we don't want to feel bad, so we search for the things that make us feel better, even if only temporarily. Then we get caught in a cycle of feeling empty, reaching for that "thing," feeling better, and then feeling empty again. Up and down we ride that rollercoaster, anticipating the exhilaration of the high that comes with feeling full and alive. Except—we always forget what comes next.

It wasn't until my late twenties that I began to recognize the cycle in my own life. I was deeply hurt by my parents' divorce and sought to fill the emptiness with relationships. In my mind, another person was what I needed to be complete. How very "Tom Cruise" of me.

If I was in a relationship, then I was fulfilled, and I put up with behaviors in partners and in myself that make me cringe now. I lost sight of myself in an effort to be pleasing to another. It took years for me to gain enough self-confidence to not be afraid of my emptiness. Once that began to happen, I could view that deep aching inside as something useful. The emptiness became a compass to gauge whether I was beginning to fall back into old habits or not. When I felt the urge to fill the void on my own, I knew I needed to redirect my course back towards God.

If only I'd had that insight two decades ago! But of course, my journey would not be what it is today without that struggle. Again, I'll quote Beth Moore from *The Quest*:

> **Isn't that often how the faith journey goes? We have to face our biggest messes and worst fears on the road to the fulfillment of God's promises to us.**[10]

Once I started the process of placing God at the center, I realized I needed to lean into Him. And I mean lean in hard. Why? Because once you are in tune with that desire for Him, there's going to be a period of uncomfortableness. If we aren't fully committed to the change then it's going to be tempting to back away.

Changing directions in life is a lot like breaking up with someone. There's the "It's not you, it's me," conversation and trying to convince your old life that you've just had a change of heart. You don't fit together the way you used to. Better to cut your losses now than to drag it out, right? (I think I just had a flashback to my last breakup, ten years ago.)

Inevitably, someone will want to get back together because it's comforting to know what we know, but that only leads us back to the rollercoaster ride we're trying to escape. Satan loves complacency. He loves to settle into our lives and convince us that the status quo is satisfying.

I knew that feeling of uncomfortableness was an indicator that God was calling me to do something outside of the plan I'd designed for my life. Perhaps you've felt this as well, and like me, you are pretending it's not there. It's that big elephant in the corner, waiting patiently for you to acknowledge it.

But God is many, many things and one of them is patient. He won't always barge in and knock everything over trying to get your attention. He waits. I've often felt like it takes destruction to get me to wake up and take notice, but the mess isn't of His making. It was my own. Do you feel like you're living in the middle of the mess right now? Toys and laundry don't count here. No amount of cleaning or reorganizing our lives is going to make the mess go away. That's because putting our wants and desires into different and prettier packaging is about as effective as trying to bail water out of the Titanic.

So, how do we know the answer to the question "What does God have planned for me?" We must embrace my least favorite four-letter word: **Wait**.

Just the thought of it makes my eye twitch. The temptation is to try and kickstart the process after praying about it once or asking a friend for advice. Don't. Resist this urge with every ounce of your being. Rolling up your sleeves and getting after it could slow down the progress you are so desperate to make. Sometimes, filling the empty space involves letting the empty space exist for a bit longer. Ironically, you may even feel the empty space get wider. What kind of cruel game is God trying to play, you ask? The truth of the matter is the void, the cavern, the empty space needs to be big enough in order for us to finally admit we aren't the ones who can fill it. I was not prepared to let go of control in my life until I saw a space so deep and so wide that I knew it would swallow me up if I took another step forward on my own.

That's the point at which you find yourself on your knees in the closet. It's only in that moment that we become ready to embrace the void and can begin to experience God's closing of the gap. In 2 Corinthians we are instructed to walk by faith and not sight, because what we see in this world is only temporary. We can waste our few years, filling them with all the pretty things or experiences that make us feel good for a little while. Or, we can embrace the emptiness we're desperately trying to fill, and live a life that is more abundantly fulfilling than we could ever imagine.

I, for one, like the idea of option two much better, but that life may not be for everyone. I know plenty of people who would prefer door number one. Based on the social media posts I see, we obviously enjoy all the stuff and showing it off to people. If everyone chose to embrace their emptiness as a good thing, what in the world would we look at on Instagram and Twitter? Now THAT'S an interesting thought. I think we'd see a whole lot less selfies and that alone would be worth it for me!

"When we take our strength from God in the seasons of sadness, others see unworldly hope and faith."

Chapter 5

Fighting an Invisible Giant

If you have kids under the age of ten, you've probably seen the movie *Moana*. A young, headstrong girl sets out across the ocean alone to restore a magical "heart" and save her island home. Along the way, she meets all sorts of crazy characters and there's plenty of singing (because, hey, it's Disney).

By far, my favorite part is when Moana meets Tamatoa, the self-centered, shiny-thing loving crab. I once heard someone describe him as a cross between David Bowie and Sebastian from *The Little Mermaid*, which does seem to hit the nail squarely on the head. Tamatoa loves to collect trinkets that make his exterior shiny, which attracts fish for his supper. He's a little bit sinister and a whole lot of funny.

His obsession with his outward appearance is a cautionary tale about what can happen to us if we allow ourselves to become distracted by all the shiny things in life. That, right there, is one of Satan's oldest tricks (just ask Eve). We are easily tempted and lured away from Christ if we are always looking for something "better." The Bible tells us in

Matthew 6:21 "for where your treasure is, there your heart will be also."

A go-to move for Satan is keeping our focus off Christ long enough to bury us in worldly distractions. At first, it all seems so innocent. For many people, it's buying new clothes, bigger houses, faster cars, expensive restaurants, or deciding where their kids should go to school. For others it's things like career success, pornography, or infidelity. Basically, it's going after anything that seems better than what we currently have.

All these things become our focus, instead of paying attention to what God wants us to focus on. Once we get distracted, it's amazingly difficult to pull ourselves back. The siren song of "stuff" is deafening in our ears. Have you noticed that in your own life? The more stuff we add onto the pile, the less fulfilled we truly are.

Why is that? Because all the stuff is tangible, for the most part. We can touch, feel, smell, and admire all the pretty things in life. It's an actual, physical distraction and God's plan for you is often blurred and hard to understand. Most of us are logical human beings, and it's easier to wrap our heads around things that can be seen rather than those that are unseen. "Stuff" can be controlled and manipulated to our liking.

This tangibility is probably the reason I'm so obsessed with home improvement shows on HGTV. Everyone is taking down walls to open up the house and adding a kitchen island to create the perfect space for entertaining.

(Who are these people doing all this entertaining, I often wonder? My idea of entertaining guests is shoving loose Legos into baskets and closing the laundry room door to make my house a little more presentable for friends. I'll admit, that's a far cry from the me of yesteryear. I've given up trying to be impressive and just let the mess show.)

When I dove head first into my network marketing business five years ago, I wanted to succeed soooo badly. I immersed myself in motivational books and "systems" for success. I probably own the entire collection of Zig Ziglar books. Instead of prayerfully considering what I was doing, and whether or not that was the best way to go about it, I took the bull by the horns and just got on with it. That's generally the way I approach things in life. If it needs to be done, just do it. If there's a better way, let's learn it (and then just do that).

Unfortunately, the temptation of success wasn't limited to the type of business I was running. As a writer, I'm faced with the comparison game daily. Someone over here is having a bunch of success and they're doing podcasts or more Facebook live videos. Oh hey, wait, look over here . . . this person has a workbook to go with their book. I must have one too!

The issue isn't with what the other person is or isn't doing. The issue is with me. My success isn't dependent on copying their formula, it lies within the specific gifts that God has given me. He designed me for His use, to impact people (not everyone, just some), and He's even gone so far as to lay out that perfect plan for me.

Satan wants to distract me with all the new ideas and ways to make things easier. I'll be laser focused on a task, when all of a sudden I'm pulled off track by a new idea. Some might diagnose me with a mild case of ADHD, but I prefer to think of myself as a squirrel.

You see, I'm a big fan of squirrels. Most people consider them to be rats with fluffy tails, but to me they're adorable outside entertainment. I love to watch them run around our backyard, chasing after each other or sprinting to the tree to escape our dog. Have you ever seen a squirrel try to cross the road? They get halfway across, stop, stand up to look around, and then sprint back the way they came. It's as if they're thinking "What's that? What am I doing here?" and then forget the original plan.

Like my furry friends, I'm easily squirreled off track and I can sense it when it happens. Things in my life begin to feel forced and then everything just grinds to a halt. I have to dig deep to avoid my squirrely moments. For me, staying consistent in my daily time with the

Lord helps keep me dialed into His promptings for me.

Know that God is making a way. In time, it will make sense even if it's beyond your imagination right now. The best thing we can do for ourselves is to spend more time tuning into the Holy Spirit, rather than praying or worrying about a decision. God knows our hearts. Our troubles and our conflicts are not news to Him. Rather than constantly seeking out new approaches or directions, practice being still and quiet. Discernment can't come when we're so loud we can't hear the small promptings showing us the way. What we have to remember is that when God urges you to "Go" or "Do," we can guarantee He's already made plans for us.

In our obedience, we are all blind men and women. Beyond feeling blind, I've felt completely without all five senses on many occasions. At first, it was not understanding the reasoning behind our battle with cancer. A parent's first instinct is to question why God would allow such a thing to happen. It was then that I began to dive deeper into His word and was compelled to gain an understanding of His promise for us:

> **And I will lead the blind in a way that they do not know, in paths that they have not known I will guide them. I will turn the darkness before them into light, the rough places into level ground. These are the things I do, and I do not forsake them. (Isaiah 42:16)**

Six months into our journey, it became obvious that I could no longer work and also give Layla the care and attention she needed. I was overcome with anxiety and doubts due to the reduced income, but God provided for that upfront. The same day I told my employer I was taking a leave of absence, a friend showed up with a check from an anonymous donor. I held that check in my hand and cried. I cried at what was ahead of us and cried at the relief that washed over me. He took away my excuse by giving me a glimpse into what He was capable of.

The more I exercise my trust in Him, the easier it becomes. It's like training for a marathon after being a couch potato. The first few weeks of running are torturous, and you continually ask yourself why on earth you're doing this, but eventually muscle memory kicks in and you do it without even thinking about it.

That's more than a metaphor. It was my actual life last summer. I was an avid runner in my twenties. Strapping on my shoes and going for a run was my favorite part of the day. It's an easy thing to do when you're young, single, and running solo. Once you bring adulting and kids into the picture things get a tad more challenging. These days, running requires a whole series of stretches and warming-up. These old muscles aren't able to make it far without a little buttering up. Not to mention there's the planning around nap schedules and packing snacks and drinks into the jogging stroller. Eventually it will stop hurting, right? Nothing like a reminder that I'm no spring chicken anymore.

Even when you get those trust muscles working again, does that mean the apprehension is completely gone? I'd be lying if I said it was. Satan never gives up trying to convince me that I'm going to fail or that I'm making the wrong choice. I still worry about having enough, and sometimes make choices based on that fear, but what is enough anyway?

For me, the fear of not having enough stems from something I perceived as trauma when I was a teenager. It seems silly as an adult, but at sixteen years old I had my checking account frozen in connection with my parent's divorce. Those two things—the sudden restriction on spending my own money and the disappearance of the safety net represented by my parents—ingrained in me that I might not have enough money one day. And thus, my instinct to save and not spend took root. Not spending sounds like a good thing, right? After all, there's a wide-spread debt epidemic going on in our culture. The saving wasn't about money though. It was about control. If I had enough money, no one could control me. I needed to be able to take care of myself.

This idea of having enough is what traps many of us in our comfort zones to begin with, and it takes humility to leave our comfort zones. It takes humility to let go of any plans you had in mind for what your life should look like, especially if it's not a real "Jesus, Take The Wheel" scenario like we had. I'll be the first one to tell you it's a whole lot easier to let God take over when the poop has hit the fan than it is when life is uneventful.

But His voice is still there. I know you hear it. Are you listening? It may not be some epic ask, like selling all your belongings and moving to a war-torn country to spread the gospel. Maybe He's simply asking you to use your time for Him more than you do for yourself. In that time with Him, he'll likely reveal a bigger ask to you. Isn't that just like God? Give him an inch and he takes a mile. But instead of acting like that neighbor who now has half your tools in his garage, or the relative who's been sleeping on your couch for a month, you'll experience His bounty ten-fold.

A word of caution to those who feel the urge to get out of your comfort zone for selfish reasons. Social media inundates us with ideas of how life should/could/would look if you made more money or had a different spouse. The mid-life crisis is a real thing and it can call to you like a siren song. People set out to "find themselves" and leave a wake of brokenness behind them.

I had what I like to call a quarter-life crisis and know all too well that living life for yourself alone is a sad existence. It feels GREAT for a while, but eventually whatever junk you ran away from in the first place will catch up with you. It will still be there, standing in front of you like a giant wall. Climb over it on your own and it will rebuild itself even higher. The longer you ignore it, the harder it is to break through . . . even if you have a giant army of undead and a zombie dragon (sorry to those of you who don't watch *Game of Thrones*).

Satan is also sneaky about influencing our emotions. Grieving people often experience what my therapist calls "grief attacks." I'll be minding my own business, having a normal day, when all of a sudden the wind gets knocked out of me. A photo, a memory, a small trinket in a drawer—and I'll find myself on my knees sobbing. Whatever I was doing or planned to do is now out the window. If you've ever suffered from anxiety or panic attacks, I'm told it's a similar experience— overwhelming emotions, brought on suddenly and without warning, that will lay you out for the rest of the day. It makes it extraordinarily difficult to function as a parent, a co-worker, or as a friend.

My layman's observation is that a type A personality is far more likely to suffer from anxiety and panic attacks due to our predisposition toward wanting control over a situation. A true type B personality tends not to get worked up because they simply aren't wired to do so. As a type A person myself, I struggle with ways to keep my sanity over the smallest of annoyances.

In 2 Corinthians, the apostle Paul tells us to fix our eyes not on what is seen, but what is unseen, because what is seen is usually the handiwork of the enemy. Not to beat a dead horse, but Satan is a crafty little fellow even if he pulls from the same playbook over and over again. He knows it's easy to knock me off track with small frustrations, like trying to open a tiny straw for a juice box. Seriously, have you ever noticed how hard it is to get those suckers open? It's like they close the plastic with super glue! Things that should be simple and straightforward really irk me when they go sideways.

In the first few days after Layla's death, I found myself sobbing over paperwork. The only thing worse than the death itself is all the paperwork that comes with it. Constantly writing out the person's name, date of birth, date of death, and social security number only reinforces the fact that they are not with you any longer. There's paperwork for the care facilities, the funeral home, and the death certificate. Then of course, there's the double-edged sword of life insurance. I used to think having life insurance on your children was morbid and a waste of money. After all, it's not the natural order of things. But now I stand corrected. And of course, the enemy has to make that process as infuriating as possible. For months, I spent parts of my week waiting on paperwork via snail-mail, sitting on hold, being transferred to the wrong department, and generally in despair over the fact that I had to keep repeating the claim was for my five-year-old daughter.

Every time I had to spend part of my day dealing with that nonsense, I could feel my blood pressure rising. That, right there, is Satan's play. If I had let my emotions run away with me, they would have derailed my entire day and turned me into the she-Hulk—making everyone I interacted with have a bad day as well.

That's not to say situations like that shouldn't make me sad or angry or upset. It's just the opposite, actually. I learned that it's important to recognize emotions as they come and allow myself to accept that it's ok to feel them. The anxiety and panic happen when I shove all those emotions down without a way to escape. Anyone who appears to have it together all the time is kidding us and themselves.

Sadness is just as much a part of life as happiness, and both can be embraced. When we take our strength from God in the seasons of sadness, others see unworldy hope and faith. Only the Holy Spirit can transform the darkness into light for someone else. Even though I hated living through my difficulties, I love how He is uniquely able to make greatness from my wreckage if I allow it.

Satan's goal is to convince us that we can take care of everything on our own. We tell ourselves that we're strong, independent, and capable of running our own lives. Oh, how I wish that were true because my twenties would have been a lot less messy if it were.

At what point in our lives do we start developing this overinflated sense of self and ego? Based on my parenting experience, I think it's around three years old. It's the age where opinions start forming and obstinance takes over. Trust me, you haven't known fury and rage until you choose the wrong color plate or cup for your child—and I'm talking about your emotions—not theirs. Their feelings go far beyond that. Was it Dylan Thomas who wrote, "Rage, rage against the color of the plate?" No? Then he obviously never dealt with a three-year-old.

From early toddlerhood, we hold fast to the idea of getting what we want, when we want it. The public tantrums tend to subside with age, contrary to what we see on Reality TV, and we learn to express our displeasure in other ways. Since the dawn of the internet age, never before has it been so easy to let the world know that you're mad at the person in the blue Camry who didn't use their blinker before cutting you off on the interstate. Then of course there's the oldie, but goodie, flipping of the bird in traffic. Yes, sir, you really showed me. Passive aggressive is generally the name of the game once we reach adulthood. Other notable favorites are: poor tipping, eye rolling, grocery cart bumping, and leaving a snarky note on the windshield.

Still, there's nothing quite like a good, old-fashioned toddler tantrum. Currently, my son's favorite way of showing me he is dissatisfied is by kicking or hitting. He's smart enough to know that kicking mommy isn't the way to go, but he shows no remorse about giving the couch or a kitchen cabinet a good whack with his plastic baseball bat. Sometimes, he prefers the light-as-a-feather-stiff-as-a-board approach, where he lays down and makes himself as immovable as possible. Or, my personal favorite, he hangs onto my legs and cries as I try my best to ignore him.

What is it about public places that seems to trigger this type of meltdown? Maybe the air is different at the grocery store than it is at home. Of course, I know that Daniel is typically hungry or tired or overwhelmed at that point, but that doesn't stop me from quietly whispering, "If you don't stop right now, Mommy is going to leave you here." Would I really? No, but there's no reason for him to know that. Although he puts on an Oscar-worthy performance, his theatrics rarely get him what he wants.

The other day, I tried an experiment where I flat-out ignored him. I went about my business, putting clothes in the dryer while he yelled demands from the staircase. "I want a banana!" The more I ignored him, the louder he got, because *clearly* I couldn't hear him. Finally, he walked downstairs into the laundry room and said, "Mommy, can I please have a banana?" Well sure, since you asked so nicely. Now if only I could get that behavior to stick.

Even if I do get a good chuckle out of Daniel's behavior, it's smart to remember that the giant Goliath also roared with laughter at David when he saw him walk up with a slingshot in his hand. This tiny person couldn't possibly defeat such a large, intimidating warrior with only a handful of rocks, could he?

So why then, do I so often find myself at the mercy of the tyrants of my own making? And I'm not just talking about my children. I have single-handedly created monsters in my life through my own well-meant efforts—things that seemed innocuous at the beginning, but quickly took on a life of their own.

Years ago, my job was one of those monsters. I could not flip the off switch on work. I obsessed over projects and deadlines and whether every detail was done exactly the right way. With the onset of the smart-phone era, this obsession became easier and easier to indulge because now I could always take work with me. Every time I heard the ding of an incoming email, I *had* to look and see what it was. Even worse, that became my expectation of others. When I didn't get an immediate response, I found myself getting annoyed at the other person's lack of commitment to their work.

My perception of commitment was unreasonable to say the least, but it took years to fully understand how I was allowing work to become a monster in my life. And how do we react when our monsters don't behave the way we want? We look for ways to make changes, again under our own power, and try harder to get them under control. When a project wasn't going the way I wanted, instead of asking for help, I poured hours into working through it on my own. But all that got me was late nights, lots of tears, and a coffee addiction.

I was talking with some friends the other day about this exact subject. I asked them, "What are the small things in our lives that seem to take over?" Technology was the immediate response. That smart phone or tablet seems to have its own gravitational pull, like the moon orbiting earth. It's constantly beckoning us to check social media or email to see what everyone else is up to.

I probed a little further, because yes, technology is one monster, but there must be others. After some thought, one friend said her time had become a monster because she had gotten to the point where it was no longer hers. Instead of prioritizing things that are important to her or allowed her a creative outlet, she is constantly saying yes to things she really doesn't want to do.

Soccer practice, dance lessons, and volunteering at school are all wonderful ways to spend your time, but not at the expense of your own sanity. Life doesn't always allow us to pick and choose exactly what we want to do, but that's what makes those few moments of downtime so precious. We need that time to recharge and reconnect with who we are as a person.

I've learned I have to ask God to help me with discernment. I have a hard time determining what's important because I have a filter of worldly views making things fuzzy. When I ask God and truly listen for His response, then my vision becomes much clearer.

I didn't always understand what discernment was. I heard the word thrown around quite a bit, but the concept never sunk in. Romans 12:2 tells us not to be "conformed to the world, but be transformed by the renewal of your mind, that by testing you may discern what is the will of God." God wants to transform us into a new person by changing the way we think. With this change, we can more clearly understand His will for us.

Although, the more we depend on God, the harder Satan tries to pull us away. Take Sunday mornings for example. Trying to get out the door for church is always a battle. Someone's lost a shoe, the dog is loose, or there's a surprise poopy diaper that has now made its way onto my dress. It seems like the enemy works double time on Sundays. He'd love it if I just put my hands up in the air and said, "Forget it! We're not making it to church this week. I give up!" Surely I am not the only one this happens to.

Leaning into God's priorities often means having to remove other things, or people, from our lives. This is rarely a popular move with those you need separation from. Those giants in our lives get louder the more we ignore them, making us want to throw in the towel on the whole thing. It takes patience on our part, and for me, a whole lot of prayer not to come undone at the slightest hiccup. Like any worthwhile journey, the perseverance pays off. Don't just climb halfway up the mountain, turn back, and miss the view from the top. We have a greater purpose on this earth—a purpose that won't be fulfilled by standing comfortably in the shade. Reflecting on Louie Giglio's words in *Goliath Must Fall* adds fuel to my internal fire:

> I have a deep conviction that the greatest regret any of us will ever know is that of standing before Jesus —knowing that we lived too safe, too comfortable, too short sighted, realizing we were gluttons for pleasure, when we were supposed to be warriors for others' freedom, and Jesus' fame.[11]

I envision the day I stand before God as the best day of my life. It's the day I'll see Layla again, and I hate to think the first thing I'll hear Him say is "Why were you so afraid? I had already defeated the giant for you."

"It's a whole lot easier to extend grace to someone when the Holy Spirit is doing the driving."

Chapter 6

The Power of Music

My musical background is pretty sparse. I have two parents that can sing, yet somehow I can't carry a tune in a bucket. Still, I took piano lessons as a kid for years, and then played the flute in elementary and junior high. My oldest sister played the flute in the high school band, so that made it super cool to me. Turns out, I was more the cheerleader type, and my music career died before I hit high school.

Even though I played an instrument for all those years, the knowledge has left my brain. Now, when I stare at sheet music, all I see are little black dots on a page. They make zero sense to me and there's no way I could play anything, even with a gun to my head. I sometimes wonder what other critical pieces of information needed to be stored when the musical parts of my brain were cleared away. I'd like to think it was some advanced math formula or literary insights from Shakespeare, but the odds are way more likely it was the theme song to Paw Patrol.

But even though I can't read music or play an instrument anymore, I've managed to retain an ear for the melodies. I'm pretty sure I could wipe the floor with the other contestants on *Name that Tune*. I hear just a few notes of a song and know what it is, so I guess all my music knowledge didn't get swept away like dust.

Music is a source of strength for me. I know many people say the same for themselves. There's a reason they've done studies on how it impacts the brain, or even how our bodies react during exercise in relation to the tempo of music. There are whole playlist suggestions for runners, walkers, cyclists, weight lifters . . . you get the picture. Each playlist is different but fitting for the needs for that sport or activity.

In my early twenties, I got hooked on indoor cycling. The biggest draw for me was not the need to get up at 5:00 a.m., but the music. Even if I was exhausted (because, again, 5:00 a.m.), as soon as that music would come on, I was focused. It's so much easier to imagine you're climbing a steep hill in the Rocky Mountains while rockin' out to Queen's "Bohemian Rhapsody."

Yes, I said Queen. They're in my top ten favorite bands of all time. Please don't think that just because I'm a Christian author I only listen to non-secular music. I do love the likes of Lauren Daigle and Casting Crowns, but I enjoy most other genres of music as well. Some of my favorite bands and solo artists include Justin Timberlake, Dave Matthews, Elton John, the Foo Fighters (Dave Grohl is the man!), Jack Johnson, Pearl Jam (really anything Eddie Vedder does), and Johnny Cash. I'm all over the board, I know.

I've had a theory for a while now that you can guess a person's age simply by what type of music they prefer. For example, someone who prefers alternative rock or heavy metal is likely in their late teens. I generally associate that type of volume and angst with hormones and the inability to recognize how loud music can do permanent damage to your ears.

Pop music, or Top 40, is a toss-up between pre-teens and their mothers. What is it about a catchy tune that can leave both a twelve-year-old girl and forty-year-old woman singing at the top of their lungs? Don't believe me? Turn on any Taylor Swift song in the middle of the mall and watch what happens.

Then there's the classic rock genre. This one is tricky because one must define what counts as classic rock. When I was growing up, this meant music by artists like Led Zepplin, Lynard Skinard, and Aerosmith (although Steven Tyler was still jamming out new records when I was in middle school). Today, radio stations try to tell me classic rock includes bands like Guns 'n Roses and Metallica. Umm . . . no. I refuse to accept that music I listened to in high school is considered classic. That's like saying my first car, a 1992 Honda Accord, is a classic. Reliable, yes. Classic, no.

Of course, I can't leave off Christian Contemporary or Christian rock music, which proves my point that I'm exactly the target audience for this genre. Late thirties to early forties mother that spends much of her time in the car with kids—that's me. There's another aspect to this group as well. At this stage in life, many of us start to have deeper life questions. I've read that for women, our twenties are when we get to figure out who we are, our thirties are for refining that definition, and our forties are when we start questioning our own definitions. We're searching for meaning as well as inspiration . . . not to mention, searching for music we don't have to turn down every ten seconds for fear our kids may hear something we'd prefer they didn't repeat at school. I mean, have you listened to some of the lyrics in songs these days? I realize that makes me sounds like an old lady and I'm fine with that.

Yes, yes, these are all gross generalizations of course. Plenty of kids enjoy classic rock and I'm sure there are men in their sixties rockin' out to T-Swift, but I hope you're seeing the point. Music has a way of defining periods in our life. I lived out my teenage years in the mid-90s, the era of grunge rock and boy bands. They're two things that could not be more different, yet equally send me down memory lane to braces, flannel shirts, and combat boots.

Back when Layla was in treatment, I spent most of our drive time to and from the hospital listening to spiritual, hopeful, and uplifting music. One of Layla's favorite artists was Mandisa, so "Overcomer" was regularly on repeat. At the time, I could take that message and channel it all day. It gave me the mental strength I needed as I held her hand during chemo or when she was sedated for radiation.

Something inside me changed after she died (I'm stating the obvious of course), and I couldn't listen to any of that for weeks. It was too painful to remember the hope and the strength I once had. I didn't need the hope because it was all over, and her miracle never came. Even now, when certain songs come on the radio, I have to change the station. Instead, I found the 90s Grunge/Alternative station on Pandora and channel some high school angst. Those were the songs on my teenage years—Pearl Jam, Live, Nirvana (although Kurt Cobain was already gone at that point).

Out of all the songs that take me back to those years, the one that always makes me stop in my tracks is "Yellow Ledbetter," again from Pearl Jam and the brilliant Eddie Vedder. I mean, seriously, you cannot even tell what the heck he's saying, but there's something about it that puts me in a trance for three minutes. Do you have a song like that? Or am I the only weirdo? Just me? . . . that's ok, I'm fine with being a weirdo.

These days I can enjoy listening to the Christian radio stations in the car again. Depending on how I'm feeling that day, I may have to turn it off before I start crying. I hate being that mom at carpool pickup who always has red eyes and a snotty nose. God did an amazing thing with my brain, though. All those songs I leaned on during treatment suddenly gained new meaning and purpose in my heart. "Praise You In This Storm," by Casting Crowns, no longer makes me think of our storm as cancer. The storm is now life without Layla. As the song says, we expected God to step up and change the situation, but the storm continued. All we heard was God's assurance that He was still with us. I have tears streaming down my face as I listen to the song right now. It takes supernatural power to face God and say, "I know you didn't give me what I want, but I'm going to praise you anyway."

That attitude is counterintuitive to our culture. When we have a bad experience, our first instinct is to tell the world via a poor Yelp review. Yep, that'll show them!

We once had a horrible (and I cannot stress enough the horrible-ness of it) experience with a contractor we hired to do some work on our home. When we bought the house we live in now, it was a hot mess. The previous owners were smokers and you could see the discolored areas around where pictures hung. The crown molding was amazing, but a disgusting yellow color, and the kitchen hadn't been touched since 1991. Fixing those were our main priorities before moving . . . paint and kitchen; the messiest jobs and not ones you want to undertake with small children in the house.

We had about four weeks to get it done before we had to be out of our current home. I got several bids on the job before deciding on one. My first mistake was not having my husband involved in the process. I know that makes me sound like a 1950s housewife, but that's just how I feel. Sorry feminists . . . take me out and shoot me now. The second mistake was not having the timeline listed in our "contract."

I'm not sure if you have much experience with home improvement, but all those people on HGTV make it look very glamorous. For the rest of us schmucks, it's frickin' stressful. Thank you Chip and Joanna Gaines for setting my expectations unreasonably high (but I still love you both!). Let me set the tone of the first day of renovation for you guys:

8:30 a.m.—I arrive at the house to meet the crew. At the time, my day job allowed me to work from home, so thankfully, I had the flexibility to do so.

9:30 a.m.—Nothing. No one had arrived, no phone call, no text. Hmmmmmm . . . I send a text and get no response.

11:00 a.m.—Now I'm annoyed. I finally get a response to my text. "Oh, we had to finish up another job this morning. We'll be there after lunch." Thanks for the heads up, dude. I guess I'll just be here whenever it's convenient for you.

At some point in the afternoon they showed up, worked for a few hours and left by about 4:00 p.m. Seems like a solid day's work (insert eye roll).

I'll save you the rest of the play-by-play, but let's just say things did *not* improve from there. After about ten days with these jokers I was ready to call it quits. My husband talked me down from the ledge, which is very unlike him. He's usually the first one to pull the plug on a project that's gone sideways. That is, he wasn't willing to fire them until one Saturday morning when I drove over to the house and realized they had been smoking inside! Remember how I said the previous owners were smokers? Somehow, that fact made these guys think it was ok for them to also smoke in our house. And they didn't even try to hide it! I have photos of their cigarette butts left strewn about the house (inside!!!!!). My blood pressure is rising as I type these words. I need to take some deep breaths y'all.

Finally, my husband was on board with a parting of ways. He called the contractor and told him he had until Monday at 10:00 a.m. to come pick up his equipment. I put a stop payment on the check I'd written him Friday afternoon (which the gentleman was not happy about). Sorry dude . . . you don't get paid two-thirds of the money when you've only done a quarter of the job.

For a few weeks, we received semi-threatening text messages saying he was going to sue us if we didn't pay him. We calmly asked him to please provide receipts for his materials and we would gladly reimburse him. We provided email and fax contact options, but never got anything. It's been over eighteen months, and no lie, I had a dream about this *last night!* Do you know how many people I've told this guy's name in an "avoid at all costs" warning? Any time a neighbor on the Nextdoor app is asking for painters, I respond with "don't hire these guys!"

All this to say that it's our nature to spread the word when we've had a bad experience. I'm sitting here scratching my head, wondering how I got on this topic in the first place, especially when I started out talking about music. I'll tie it back together somehow, Scout's honor.

There is no way I would have said to this person, "You know what . . . you did a terrible job, but I'm still going to give you a glowing review on the internet." There may be people in this world who would do that because they hate to say a bad word about anyone, but that ain't me (yes, I said ain't . . . I'm from Texas. It's a word here.)

But that tendency to warn others about our bad experiences does not stop with home improvement or poor restaurant service. I have seen brokenhearted people drop their beliefs and faith like a hot potato. If there was a place to leave reviews about God on Yelp, I guarantee it would be filled with dissatisfied customers. One-star reviews abound because people didn't get what they wanted, when they wanted it. "Don't use this guy . . . He never fulfills His promises," or, "We waited and waited, but never heard back," is what I imagine they'd say. And really, who can blame them? It takes a deeeeep rooted belief in the Holy Spirit and all that God is capable of to still praise him during the storm. I've sat here for more than an hour trying to think of the words to describe what that feels like—to have the desire to say, "I love you God, even though my daughter died." It's not human to feel that way. THAT is how I know the Holy Spirit exists and lives inside of me.

Sometimes I wonder what songwriters are thinking as they write the amazing verses that speak to us so deeply. When Lauren Daigle wrote "Trust in You," what was she experiencing in life? What was her mountain that didn't move? Still, she knows that God is always good and His ways are better than ours. She acknowledges that her miracle did not come, but she knows exactly where her faith and trust lie. The song is a beautiful interpretation of Deuteronomy 31:8:

> **The Lord himself goes before you and will be with you; He will never leave you nor forsake you. Do not be afraid; do not be discouraged.**

Let's just be honest for a quick second, okay? It is HARD to not be discouraged during the troubles we face. Discouragement comes from so many different places in life, and somehow we feel better when there's a specific thing or person to blame.

I have a person in my life who is a chronic complainer. Do you have one of those? No matter what the situation is, they have a complaint. If you're unsure whether your person is a chronic complainer, here are a few ways you can identify these people.

First, there are always issues at work. Their job history is littered with "bad managers" and back-stabbing coworkers. Someone is always out to get them, which makes it impossible for them to stay at one job for an extended period of time. If they do manage to stay employed, it's not without drama. Second, nothing is ever their fault. Their lack of motivation or ability to be on time is simply a product of a problem someone else created. Third, everything is personal. It's genuinely difficult to share insights or constructive criticism with this person without it being interpreted as a blitz attack. Needless to say, this person also has trouble with relationships.

I believe the root of the issue is an inability to deal with discouragement in our lives. Unfortunately, life doesn't always give us a scapegoat when it comes to our problems. Sometimes the problem is us, and that's a tough pill to swallow. But when we open our hearts to the Holy Spirit, he starts the work for us.

Surrendering to Him changes our perspective. Our hearts become softer towards others, and we see them differently as we begin to see them through Christ's eyes. It's a whole lot easier to extend grace to someone when the Holy Spirit is doing the driving. Who else needs to get out of the driver's seat and avoid the temptation to be a backseat driver? Am I the only one raising my hand here?

Those of you with teenagers can relate a little bit, I'm sure. Teaching your kids to drive must be a similar adventure, although one I have yet to have the pleasure of experiencing. "Adventure" is a nice way of saying "scares-the-pants-off-of-you" experience. You sit in the passenger's seat, while gripping the door and pushing the imaginary brake on your side.

We have to stop pushing the imaginary brakes, folks. God knows the direction we need to go and He's fully capable of steering us the right way. He even knows how to drive a 5-speed, which is more than I can say for myself. (That was a traumatic experience I'd rather not talk about. Oh, the horrors that were seen in that empty parking lot in 1996. The skid marks on my soul still remain.) But with God in control, there will be no fender benders. It's more like taking a road trip with your best friend. You have the top down on the convertible and your hair is blowing in the wind. Your biggest worry is where to stop for breakfast tacos. Ok, so maybe I'm taking it a step too far, but your trip through life will be so much nicer when you let Him do the driving. Our job should just be to pick the soundtrack! May I suggest a little Pearl Jam?

"There's no way to get rid of the pain other than letting it be felt and working through the healing."

Chapter 7

Pardon the Disruption

I still remember sitting in church only a few weeks after Layla's relapse and hearing our pastor, Pete Briscoe, say, "When the Holy Spirit does something in your life, it will be disruptive."

Amen, brother, I whispered under my breath. I have been more disrupted in the past two years than any other time I can remember in my life. And my life hasn't been all sunshine and rainbows either. My parents divorced when I was thirteen. I've been through multiple breakups, a failed marriage, and moved to four different states in two years. All of this happened before the age of twenty-five. In my mind, I was pretty good at rolling with the punches and moving on, but in hindsight I can see where all of that only provided an inflated sense of ego. Or, as my three-year-old says, "I can do it myself!"

Once my life was completely disrupted in a way that I couldn't control, I was open and vulnerable. I had lost my sense of security and my sense of self with one uttered word: cancer. The time of doing it all myself was now over, but the idea of asking for help was absolutely foreign to me. My entire adult life had been focused on how I was going to make things happen, how I was going to work it all out.

Hanging in my home office are three quotes: "Make it happen," "Don't Give Up," and "It's hard to beat a person who never gives up."

Looking at them now, the irony of it is not lost on me. I've never really done anything on my own, except maybe carrying ALL the grocery bags in with one trip. Oh sure, I've forced myself to the point of exhaustion with the idea that I'm "doing it," but who am I kidding? Myself, obviously.

Even the little things in life go so much more easily when we've surrendered to the idea that our source of strength does not come from our own sheer will. In 2 Corinthians 4:8, Paul's letters make it abundantly clear that our strength and power is from God and not us:

> **We are hard pressed on every side, but not crushed.**

We're sort of like superheros when we harness the strength God has placed within us. Within His will, there is nothing that can stop us from our task. That doesn't mean we get a free pass in life to take a stroll down Easy Street. In fact, the opposite is often true, but our willingness to let go of our old ways will result in abundance.

One of the habits I tried to restart the summer of Layla's relapse was going for a walk or run most mornings. I'd gained about ten pounds during the time Layla was inpatient for chemo and, for me, that's a slippery slope I didn't want to find myself going down. So, early in the morning before the kids got up or immediately after everyone had breakfast, I'd load up the stroller with water and snacks and we'd hit the trail.

The thing I love most about our city is that it has an amazing set of walking and biking trails, and the one closest to our house has a playground immediately adjacent to it. Once I finished my walk, we'd stop at the playground for the kids to burn off some energy before the heat of the day. That is the goal of basically every stay-at-home-mom with young kids, but I thought I was clever because I had never been a stay-at-home-mom before. Wear the kids out before lunch and they'll take better naps, leaving mommy with more time for doing all the other things that have to be done—exciting things like loading the dishwasher, folding laundry, and getting the gum unstuck from the back of the car seat.

After a few weeks of getting back on the exercise wagon, I mentioned to Bryan that I probably needed to buy new running shoes. I can always feel my knees taking more of a beating once the support has worn out. The shoes I normally wear are not inexpensive and I really didn't want to spend the money on new ones, so I continued to put off the purchase.

Fast forward to a few days later, and a package arrived addressed to me. We had been receiving a ton of boxes for our Christmas in July Toy Drive, so it wasn't unusual to have four or five packages arrive each day. We were keeping the UPS man busy. Bryan opened the box thinking it was more toys and calls to me from the other room, "Your shoes are here." Shoes? I didn't order any shoes, did I? Was I sleep-shopping on Amazon again? I walked over to see what the heck he was talking about, and sure enough, there were a brand-new pair of Nike Frees in a beautiful lilac color. What the heck? Where did those come from? Then I remembered a completely random text message I had received about a week before. A friend had asked what size shoe I wore. I replied that I wore size eight, but didn't have time to follow up with "Why?" and then promptly forgot all about it.

What's the big deal about shoes? Because, my friends, God provided. Yes, I know, they're just shoes, but for me it was so much more. This was a small need, one that frankly I could have lived without, but God showed me that he was going to take care of even the little things. In a life that felt crazy and out of control, He was showing me that this disruption in our lives did not mean the end of His ability to take care of us, even in the smallest of ways.

Do you ever try to control the little things in life because you feel like God has bigger things to worry about? First of all, that's ridiculous because God doesn't worry about anything. He knows all. He IS all. Second, it's the little things where we can see God working most of all.

> **Great is our Lord and mighty in power; his understanding has no limit. (Psalm 147:5)**

It's easy to fall into the habit of trusting God with only the "big" things in life, like our health, our family life, and our jobs. But at what point do we draw the line between big and small? Eventually we find ourselves working to manage and fix everything in our lives. Surely God isn't concerned with our boring, everyday troubles, we think.

What I've experienced in this season of life is that if we can't (or won't) allow God to take care of even the smallest things, we're going to struggle to trust Him with the big things. We can't turn on the Bat Signal to call God into our lives only when things get too big for us to handle ourselves. He is always there, always present, always willing to care for us. Instead of working on fixing and managing, we should be surrendering every moment.

> **Behold, I am the Lord, the God of all flesh; is anything too difficult for me? (Jeremiah 32:27)**

Not even the smallest need is overlooked when we allow God to work in our lives. Not even a need for new running shoes. For me, those shoes were a reminder that, no matter what, we are taken care of. We are loved beyond imagination. I've experienced Him providing in the smallest ways, so I know I can trust Him with the most important things. One of the things I'm reminded of, when thinking about those new shoes, is how tired I was during that time.

We had been out of inpatient chemo for months, but the stress of it all was still clinging to me. At least, I thought that was the case. I was actually three or four weeks pregnant, and had no idea! Talk about a major disruption to our lives! A third child was not something we had planned or really even thought about. We had a girl and a boy and that completed our little family of four. Let this be a lesson to you all, gentlemen. Follow up with the doctor after the initial consultation and have the actual vasectomy done. Of course, we know now there's a very good reason why that didn't happen. Our surprise third child, Evelyn Jo Rose, was part of God's plan because He knew what was headed our way. Looks like being tired is still in my foreseeable future.

I'm not sure there's even a word to describe the amount of tired that I was at that time. Exhausted, weary, zonked, enervated (that's a five-dollar word!)—none of those seem to do it justice. I'm sure every parent has felt completely exhausted at some point. It usually starts about the time baby is born and I'm told it lasts through high school. I don't mean to say that people who aren't parents don't get tired. Everyone has their "stuff" that wears on them, but I can only speak from my perspective and that's as a parent of small children. Not just a parent . . . a mom. Yes, dads get tired too. And if you're a single dad, then I'll lump you in with the moms on this one. But I think if the topic "Name Another Word for Tired" came up on Family Feud, the survey would say "MOTHER."

I still remember how tired I was when the kids were itty bitty babies and I'd be up four or five times a night nursing and rocking them. I had no concept of time except whether the sun was out or not. Days of the week didn't matter or even exist. One time, when Daniel was about six weeks old and had slept a few good stretches over several days, I looked at Bryan and said, "I think I could do this one more time" (as in, have a third baby). He looked me straight in the eye and said, "You're drunk on sleep." Maybe that was what jinxed us? Sure enough, that stretch of blissful six hours of sleep a night vanished as quickly as it came. I had gotten cocky and angered the sleep gods! Pretty sure I'm still paying for that one.

Being physically tired kind of goes with the territory when you have little kids. Their sleep is erratic, they wake up at ungodly hours in the morning, and will literally fight you about going to bed. All of a sudden there's an emergency snack situation or they're dying of thirst, like they've gone without food or water all day. They're insane little monsters.

This tiredness I was feeling went beyond just physical. It was a weariness deep in my soul. I was restless in every part of my life. Things that once made me feel fulfilled, left me empty and wanting more.

This was the rumblings of a disruption I wasn't quite ready to face. I really liked my job. I was good at it and had been with the same company for over sixteen years. Frankly, it was the longest relationship I'd ever had and leaving felt like having to break up with someone I loved. I prided myself in being an excellent colleague and team member, but at the end of every day I asked myself "Why?" I felt a calling to do more. To share more with others and to make more of an impact in this fight against childhood cancer. I also felt a prompting to write and tell others about the amazing way God has carried us through an unthinkable time. I want everyone to know He will do the same for them.

Maybe you feel a longing in your heart, too? Cancer or writing may not be your calling, but you've got awesomeness to share with the world! What keeps us from doing it? We rationalize that it would be irresponsible to quit our jobs so we can be happy and pursue our dreams, which to some extent is true. You and the people in your family probably like to eat and put gas in the car. How do you pull the trigger on something when you can't see what the outcome will be? Things like insurance and car payments and groceries really put a kink in the plan for feeling fulfilled, don't they?

So, what's the answer? What do we do when our souls are tired and need new life? I think the answer is much simpler than many self-help books want us to think. The answer is rest. Not physical rest, although I'll take some of that as well, but soulful rest.

What the heck is that? For a person who enjoys being in control, that's the hardest part to grasp because it looks different for everyone. At the center of it all is a close relationship with Christ. Over and over I have tried to manage life with my own efforts, always falling short of what I truly desire. "I've got this" are the three worst words in the English vocabulary (followed closely by "watch this" and "hold my beer"). Those are the words you will generally hear in one of two situations:

1. Your toddler (child, teenager, or drunk adult) is about to jump off/lift/or otherwise attempt something ridiculously stupid, OR;
2. YOU are intent on doing something and you're convinced you don't need help from anyone.

Either way, failure (and in case of #1, physical harm) is imminent.

It wasn't until this cancer journey was thrust upon us that I understood what it was to surrender to Christ—to surrender to the idea that I literally have no control over the situation, but He has ultimate control. It's the most uncomfortable feeling I've ever had. Maybe you've felt it too? Giving up control was like giving up breathing for me, but giving up that control has also brought me a peace in life that I had never before experienced.

It seems counterintuitive since I often feel my life is the furthest thing from peaceful, but I *know* He has parted the waters for our family and I *know* he has moved mountains we'll never know about. I don't need to move them myself and neither do YOU! I want to wake up every morning with a reminder of that truth, because if I don't stand firmly in that space the tiredness will creep back in and try to overwhelm me. I'd much rather live in a space of peace, wouldn't you?

Every day I witness people in all walks of life who have given up hope and are living a life without Christ. Everything in their life has fallen apart: their relationships, careers, and families are in utter shambles. Some are still trying to hold the illusion of a perfect life together by shoving any evidence of their disasters into the proverbial closet. It's heartbreaking to see them struggle, standing alone in the ruins of their lives. Why do they feel the need to keep covering it up? Because the mess is what scares people. It's easier to smile and put a pretty cover over our troubles than to let the door on the closet stay wide open. Sure, things may fall out from time to time, but that's life.

It reminds me of the signs you can buy at Hobby Lobby that say, "Pardon the mess . . . our children are making memories."

Even in jest, we need to make excuses for what is a normal part of life. If someone in your life can't handle your mess, then maybe it's time to assess whether or not that person is really your kind of people. Some days the closet door is going to be wide open, and you won't have the energy to kick all the junk back inside. I say, come inside, and watch your step. This is just what it looks like most days.

Disruption leads to mess which often leads to pain. Pain is an interesting notion, isn't it? We use the word to cover all manner of topics: physical, emotional, financial, spiritual. Each person has a specific level of tolerance for pain. Science tells us that women, in particular, have a higher level of pain tolerance (yes! it's science!) for doing things like birthing babies. Have you seen those videos of men experiencing simulated contractions? I mean, come on, there's no doubt women were designed for pain!

All joking aside, as humans we do all we can to avoid pain. It's a survival mechanism. Pain = slowing down and slowing down = death. Pain is not so dramatic these days, but thousands and thousands of years ago it would have been. When we hurt, we're forced to heal, at least that's the concept. Why then, do so many of us simply try to cover up the pain instead of embracing it and allowing the healing to happen?

We can't be bothered with the downtime or the disruption to our everyday lives. For physical pain, we take pharmaceuticals to numb ourselves, but then that numbness becomes a way of life and we don't know how to function without it. When we experience emotional pain, we stuff ourselves full of (*insert your favorite coping mechanism here*). For some people, that's food or shopping or work or our kids or exercise. If there's financial pain, pull out the credit card or take out another loan in order to avoid addressing the pain and finding a new lifestyle. Then there's spiritual pain and this one is a doozie. Most people are so busy trying to avoid all the other pain they don't even realize there's spiritual pain. Pain, numb, repeat. Pain, numb, repeat. More of us live this way than don't. I know I have for a long time.

I remember how different my birth experiences were between Daniel and Layla. I had had an emergency c-section with Layla, and wanted a natural birth with Daniel, but ended up with a second c-section. My experience the first time around wasn't awful, so I thought I knew what to expect. What I hadn't considered the second time was the x-factor, already having one child to chase around! Instead of relaxing during the evenings and weekends, binge watching TV and feeding the baby, I was trying to breastfeed with one arm and help the toddler wipe her hiney with the other. To this day, I still consider that my most proud "new mom of two" moment! I counted down the minutes until I could take my next pain pill, because I would go-go-go while I was numb, but once it started to wear off, it was ow-ow-owwww!!! The numbness of the pain pills allowed me to ignore the fact that my body was trying to heal, and in order to heal I needed to REST! Rest has always been a four-letter word to me, just ask my husband. In my mind, if you're resting, you're being lazy because there's always something to do.

Not that long ago, I picked up a copy of *Present Over Perfect* by Shauna Niequist. I'm probably the last woman on earth to read this book (or at least it seems), but I deeply identify with her struggle and where she found herself before she wrote the book. I fake rested. all. the. time. I said yes to too many things, I worked hard out of fear, and I never gave my full attention to just one thing. And friends, I needed a rest. It was freeing to read that I wasn't the only one experiencing this in life.

Isn't it fantastic when someone understands your pain? We're freed from the burden of being "different" or "high maintenance" when someone else says "YES! Me too!" But we don't share our burdens, do we? We all silently agree that it's just "life" and life is exhausting. We post pictures of our smiling faces on Instagram and Facebook and tell everyone how much fun we're having, but on the inside, we're weeping because we're so tired. We need rest and healing and we have no idea where to find that.

Consider the child who needs a nap and is crying for no logical reason. As parents, we say, "Oh, he/she is over-tired. They need a nap." But getting the child to nap is a feat within itself. Once we're past the point of exhaustion, our bodies practically refuse the rest that it's asking for! It makes no sense! Our bodies weren't designed to go until they break, we were designed for regular rest. So, please hear me on this—GO TAKE A NAP!

Even if you're still trying to pretend you aren't physically tired, I can almost guarantee your soul is. One morning last summer I woke up and God was practically yelling at me. "What are you doing? Why won't you stop and rest!? I'm telling you to STOP!" He had been whispering it for a long time. Even before cancer came into our lives, he tried to show me, but I never listened. I had too much fear about what that would look like. I couldn't use the "R-word."

I listened and I stopped, and then I found myself asking, "Ok, what now?" See how I did that? I stopped doing what I was doing, but immediately started asking what to do next. I'm tricky, but God sees through me.

"Live in me," is what He requested. Without anything else to go on, I picked up my Bible and a new Bible study. Instead of rushing through it and squeezing it in around other activities like I normally would, I treated it like it was my job. The study was in the Gospel of John and called *Proven: Where Christ's Abundance Meets Our Great Need*, by Jennie Allen.[12] To be honest, I was expecting a study on how to trust God's love for me and allow it to meet my needs instead of trying to meet them on my own. I expected this because that's basically what it says on the back of the book. Surprisingly, though, this study was actually about disruption and pain! At least that's what God began to reveal to me through it. Lots and lots of pain, but pain with a purpose.

When Layla was first diagnosed, it was relatively easy to see how this (temporary) pain could be a wonderful testimony to God's grace and healing. Bryan and I saw our community rally around us, relieving us of burdens and coming together to show us how much our family was loved. God provided us with the right people at the right time to show us His presence and how he had covered for all of our fears. There was no need for pain because it was all good. We both experienced transformations that never would have happened except for cancer, but we weren't done yet. The pain came back and stayed. Now I see that October 2016 was just the warm up. It was when we started to flex our faith muscles, but then we got a little lazy. Our faith started to look like a Lifetime Fitness around February 5, when the resolutions wear off. We needed to get back to the gym.

If we can embrace the disruption of pain and begin to peel back our layers, we allow the pain to do its job. It helps us slow down and heal, and to do this without fear of what's to come. I know it hurts when we pay attention to the pain in life. It's easier to push it or numb it away, but those tricks always wear off. There's no way to get rid of the pain other than letting it be felt and working through the healing. And that brings more pain. Pain. Heal. Repeat. How exciting and freeing is that!

"He cannot be crushed by the weight of it and we must be willing to hand over that burden to Him today and every day."

Chapter 8

Anger Management

Have you ever watched a small child fly into a rage? We call them tantrums because it sounds cuter, but it's really rage. They can't help it because their poor little minds haven't developed enough to regulate those emotions, so it's up to us adults to help them navigate the situation. Problem is, most adults still can't navigate their own feelings, let alone a tiny human's. During a grief counseling session, my therapist and I got onto the topic of anger and bitterness. It's a normal part of grief (and life really) to have feelings of anger. Under it all, at the very, very bottom, there's usually grief. But most people don't recognize it. That's because grief isn't just for people mourning a death or a loss. It's not an empty table with a reserved sign on it waiting for the next customer.

Anger is a funny emotion because people aren't usually angry just to be angry. Anger almost always sits on top of sadness, fear, or anxiety. So many of us live in one of those three chronic states day in and day out. But what are we afraid of? For some, it's fear of losing a job and not being able to pay bills or feed our family. For others, it's the FOMO (that means fear of missing out for those of you who do not speak millennial). Sadness can creep in so many ways. Whether we're mourning the loss of a relationship, a friend, a family member, or the life you thought you would have. Social media is so often the trigger by telling us we aren't measuring up to the photos we see. Why doesn't our life match what everyone else seems to have?

Then there's anxiety. What would it be like to know a life without anxiety? To be freed from the worry that every phone call carries bad news about a loved one or that the other shoe is always about to drop. How would we live our lives differently?

My whole life, I've been what I call an "apocalyptic worrier." I can take any small situation and imagine the absolute worst outcome possible. I considered it a coping mechanism for a long time. If my brain could wrap itself around the worst possible thing, then surely, I could survive whatever happened. But the worst thing DID happen to our family and I was not prepared. You cannot possibly prepare yourself to help your four-year-old child battle cancer. Even if cancer is not your situation, anxiety can paralyze you from moving forward in life. What if you take the wrong job? Are you paying enough attention to your kids? Would it be better if you stayed at home instead of working? Would it be better if you went back to work? These are just a few of the thoughts that have kept me up over the years as a working mom.

I've always been in awe (and slightly jealous) of the Trappist Monks who live in absolute silence for most of their lives. First off, they get to wear robes all day. I could totally get on board with that because most days putting on yoga pants seems like a task. This could also be due to the fact that, as I write this, I'm 38 weeks pregnant and putting on any type of clothing leaves me out of breath. And forget about shoes. Thank goodness for the warm weather in Texas this February, or else I'd be dropping Daniel off at school barefoot.

Secondly, the monks don't have to talk. That may seem strange coming from someone who seems to have a lot to say on paper, but as an introvert, speaking to people out loud for long periods of time is exhausting. I will absolutely do it when necessary, especially if it means I get to speak about what God has laid on my heart, but I promise I will be plumb worn out after the fact.

Last, but not least, I have to wonder whether or not those monks ever feel worried or anxious. They're seemingly free from the burdens of the world around them. Their existence is quiet, so no nagging or crying toddlers to contend with. What in the world do they do all day?

In case you are wondering too, a quick Google search will let you know. It says they don't necessarily take an explicit vow of silence, but they only speak when necessary—things like working together to get a job completed efficiently (also something I can get on board with), speaking about their spiritual progress, or occasionally a friendly conversation. I'm going to assume this is not the same type of friendly conversation that goes on when my girlfriends and I go out for dinner. All-in-all, it doesn't sound like a bad gig to me.

Since that type of lifestyle isn't in the cards for most of us, is it possible for us to have that sort of peace in our lives? I absolutely believe it is if we're willing to accept that the peace beyond all understanding lives within our hearts already (Philippians 4:7). The Holy Spirit has placed it there for those of us who believe and have accepted that Jesus Christ is our savior. I have felt it many times and I'm always amazed at what it feels like to be at peace when I should be raging against the world. It truly is beyond all human understanding. So, if it's free for the taking and it's within us already, then how come our world doesn't look more like that of a Trappist Monk's?

Speaking from personal experience, I frankly didn't know that peace was there. I hate to beat this whole "control issues" topic like a dead horse, but hey, that's why you bought the book, right? If I never felt like peace was available outside of my own efforts, then why would I assume it was already available in my heart? When I was pushed to the limit of what I could mentally and physically do about my problems, it was like a little switch went off in my brain. I can only assume the Holy Spirit flipped it because, like I said, I had no idea it was there. I'm certain it originated from some wonderful person who was praying for me to find peace about our situation and their prayer was surely answered. So, thank you, whoever you are.

If we consider my story to be like most others, and also the fact that Christians don't realize the peace that lives within them, I can only be amazed that people hold it together in polite society as well as they do. I often look around at a place like Starbucks and wonder who's about to snap. Is it me? Am I one *"Sorry, ma'am, that was the last pumpkin loaf"* away from completely losing it in public? Maybe that's why we're so exhausted all the time?

We expend the majority of our energy on just holding the pieces of our sanity together with an Elmer's glue stick. For those of you not familiar, glue sticks aren't that great at holding a whole lot together. There's a definite shelf life, equaling the distance from the preschool door to your car. At that point, it all falls apart and tears ensue because the precious craft is now ruined. And your kid is usually pretty upset, too.

Am I the only one who wonders what's happening with all this anger roaming around? Most of us hold it in because we have no space to let it go. Speaking as a parent, our kids often suffer as a result. When we're angry, even the littlest thing can set us off. After a long day of work and stress, one more "Mommy . . . mommy . . . mommy . . . mommy . . . watch this," can send us over the edge. When that happens to me, I look down at that sweet face, now stained with tears, and it's like a knife in my heart. Why did I do that? He didn't deserve to be yelled at. All he wanted was to tell me about his day. Ugh, mommy guilt times infinity!

It's comforting to know I'm not the only one who has these thoughts. A few months before Layla passed away, Bryan and I had a hilarious talk over lunch. He told me he wanted to open a business where people could come and destroy things. In my mind, I started replaying the movie *Office Space*, where the guys take the printer out in the field and smash it with bats. It sounded like a great idea to me! It sure as heck is cheaper than therapy, but it was a small spoiler to realize places like that already exist. I guess we're not all that creative.

I could tell Bryan had hit a wall of emotions. He was tired of each day being the same. He was angry at cancer and I was too. Unfortunately, we hadn't even gotten to the hard part, but we didn't know that at the time. I'm thankful that, at that point, we were both ahead of the curve when it came to identifying our anger.

So, instead of opening up a business to smash #allthethings, Bryan instead resorted to taking out his rage on a tree in our backyard. We never liked the tree to begin with. It provides no shade or real functionality except for leaving a mess on our driveway and cars every spring. And so, late at night, I often heard the whack-whack-whack of an axe against the tree. I have to give credit to the tree. It's still hanging in there, unbothered by the abuse it's received. Which, honestly, is a little disappointing because now I have to endure another spring of sticky mystery substance all over most things in the backyard, including the children.

Why is it that people don't let go of their anger? Are we so used to the feeling that it doesn't even phase us anymore? We stay all bottled up until one day, some poor person at Target doesn't put their cart back and gets the brunt of what you've been holding in for days (or weeks or years). I can still feel myself on the verge of it some days. All my tears are waiting to spill over, yet I force myself to hold them back—not always, but most of the time. A few days after Layla passed away, I decided to go to the grocery store. I'm not sure who allowed me to do this, but nevertheless, I went. Friends, let me just tell you, if another friend is in mourning and they want to venture out alone, DO NOT LET THEM. You hop in that car, preferably driving, and go with them.

I mostly walked around in a daze grabbing random foods, and then headed to the checkout line. The lady in front of me was writing a check. (I'm going to apologize to all you lovely people who still write checks at the grocery store. You are wonderful and sweet, so please ignore the rest of this story.) Let's just say that I worked hard to keep my wits about me, but there was definitely some misplaced rage boiling over. I mean, who writes a check? I kept saying to myself, "Don't end up on the news, don't end up on the news." I could see it all in my head, "Local pregnant woman tackles grandmother at grocery store—story at ten o'clock!"

To top off the frustration on that trip, as I was putting groceries in the trunk, I witnessed a man leave his cart two feet from the cart return. I thought my head was going to explode. "Don't worry sir," I shouted at him. "I'll put it back for you!" He turned and gave me a strange look and walked a little faster to his car. "Yeah . . . you keep walkin' mister," I muttered under my breath. "You know what you did. I hope your car gets scratched." I promise, I'm actually a really nice person who doesn't usually act that way. Grief made me do it!

That particular episode happened right before Thanksgiving, and the approaching holiday season didn't help the situation at all. It's bad enough to deal with all the stress and pressure between November and January, but throw grief onto the pile and you might as well have lit a match on dry leaves. On Christmas Day, we took a break from watching *A Christmas Story* on twenty-four hour repeat, and found ourselves watching the strong man contest on ESPN instead. Ya know . . . because nothing says Christmas like very large men lifting trucks and stuff.

One of the signature events of the contest is the Atlas stones. Basically, these guys have to pick up huge, heavy stones, carry them across a specific distance and then place them on pedestals. The kicker is 1) there's more than one stone and; 2) each one gets progressively heavier and the pedestal gets taller. Oh, and 3) they're round . . . so that makes picking them up, carrying, and manipulating them that much more difficult. Have you ever tried to carry a bunch of balls at once? It's much more challenging than squares. So, as I watched this, I thought to myself "THIS is how I feel right now." Like I was carrying around this huge boulder, basically on my chest, but I had nowhere to put it down. No one could take it from me or carry it for me. We all have burdens that leave us angry, weary and tired, those things in life that no one else knows about but weigh us down daily. Guilt, shame, regret, heartache. God knows. He sees our hearts and there's no judgement, just his deep desire for us to put it down and hand it over to Him. He cannot be crushed by the weight of it and we must be willing to hand over that burden to Him today and every day.

> **Praise be to The Lord, to God our Savior, who daily bears our burdens. (Psalm 68:19)**

We weren't built to carry that weight around. It's not what God intended for us, yet most of us feel an obligation to do so. Why? Either because we don't know any better or because of pride. For me, pride is almost always the culprit. I'm strong. I'm a mom. I can do all things, with coffee. That false confidence strengthens me. It is the sacrilegious battle cry of control freaks everywhere. But our strength does not come from ourselves. No matter what your circumstances are, no one is out of God's reach. His strength is widely available to those who can put pride aside and admit they cannot do it alone. Sometimes, we even need help finding the strength to take that first step and let go of our pridefulness. Is that even a word? If not, it should be.

What is it that you pride yourself on? Do you wear a particular trial as a badge of honor even though it's literally crushing you? Does it bring out feelings of anger and bitterness because you feel like you're the only one up to the task? Why do we do that to ourselves? I realize I'm asking a lot of questions here, but our motivations need to be examined. How can we be proud of something that also brings us to a raging point? Or if not rage, at least annoyance and a simmering vexation.

I can, of course, use myself as an example. I love folding bed sheets. I pride myself on the fact that I can fold a fitted sheet like nobody's business, thank you Martha Stewart. But even as I settle in to enjoy the process, I begin feeling annoyed that no one else in my household can do this. Why am I the only one folding laundry, I begin to ponder. There's actually no truth to that statement because my husband does, in fact, fold laundry from time to time, but he's not a fitted sheet folder extraordinaire like myself. And should I expect him to be? Did he spend hours watching YouTube videos to learn? Nope, that was just me.

Another ridiculous skill I pride myself on is knowing the most efficient way to get anywhere (self-proclaimed, of course). How could someone not be an expert at this with the abundance of traffic navigation phone apps that are available? Talk about something that brings out the anger in people. Hell hath no fury like someone getting cut off on the interstate. It's almost ironic. If we'd get off our phone and pay more attention, there'd be fewer accidents and less need to figure out and avoid where all the traffic backups are. Google Maps gives you at least three options, and there are any number of apps specifically designed to navigate you around hazards that might delay you more than five minutes. Stalled car on the tollway? Ain't nobody got time for that!

Whether it's driving or just walking in the mall, my brain is constantly on high alert for "hazards" that might slow me down. Elderly couple at three o'clock, steer away to the other side of aisle. Maybe one day I'll slow down and enjoy a leisurely stroll through the mall, but with one or more kids in tow, this lady is on a mission to get in and get out! And why am I at the mall anyway? If Amazon Prime doesn't carry it, I'm certain I don't need to buy it.

When it comes to navigation, my husband and I are exact opposites. There are many times I sit in the passenger seat, mostly holding my tongue, thinking to myself, *Why is he going this way? Doesn't he know this way has the most stoplights?* He honestly isn't bothered by spending an extra ten or twenty minutes in the car, and I firmly believe this is because he doesn't often have screaming children in the backseat. As he drives around the city all day for work, he has the luxury of listening to the radio (whatever station he wants!) and walking into a restaurant instead of pulling through the drive-through.

Since I've gotten on the topic of traffic somehow, I have to ask whether I'm the only one who's noticed that it always seems to take longer the first time you travel somewhere new? I always assumed it was just me, but apparently, it's a real phenomenon. It's called the "return trip effect," and since it's on the internet, it must be real. I'm sure it's something only recently discovered since once upon a time people actually took the scenic route (crazy, right?). Driving through small towns on two-lane roads was considered part of the fun. Not my kind of fun, but it was someone's entertainment. When is the last time you took a trip and thought, "Which way will take us through the most speed traps!"? (I mean—small towns.) That probably hasn't happened since you were a kid and your parents were doing the driving. Perhaps as my children get older I'll start to appreciate taking the long way, if only to torture them with more quality time with the family in the car.

You see, the problem with obsessing over the fastest route is two-fold. First, you spend a whole lot of energy deciding your route, only to be sorely disappointed when you hit road construction (because in Texas there is ONLY road construction). Secondly, you miss all the good stuff, like the world's largest ball of yarn or Barney Smith's Toilet Seat Art Museum in San Antonio. Seriously folks, I can't make this stuff up!

I can attest to the fact that there is real value in taking the long way around. It's quieter and less white-knuckled-on-the-steering-wheel frantic. That's how I would describe my current situation in life—slower, quieter, unplanned, with no expectations. I wish this was a path I had chosen voluntarily long ago, but I've never been good at being told what to do, having patience for doing things the slow way, or even for people who do things the slow way. Being stuck behind a slow driver still easily elicits a visceral response from me as I feel my blood pressure on the rise. This journey of learning to let go of what I cannot control has revealed to me that when you're frantically searching for the best, most efficient way, you're usually not thinking about God's way. God's way is rarely quick, much to my dismay, but it's always better than what I could ever plan.

God's way is not always without frustration and anger though. It rarely comes without some sort of major uncomfortableness. Sticking with what's familiar isn't difficult until you're forced to face an unimaginable life change. We live our lives in a never-ending loop of the "return trip effect." We stay in jobs that leave us unfulfilled because we're too afraid to trust where God is calling us. The logistics of finances and "making it work" are too overwhelming to process. It's easier to stay comfortably numb and make the same commute day in and day out.

I say all of this as I'm currently smack dab in the middle of this dilemma, wrestling every day with what choice I'll make after my maternity leave runs out. Will I go back to comfortable or step out in faith to something entirely new and, frankly, frightening? The old me is lobbying hard to make a plan so that the new path feels comfortable before I even set foot on it, but the new me knows that's not how it works.

It's going to be uncomfortable to give up control and let God work, but it's the only way to truly experience what He's working on for me. Looking in my basket, I see only enough bread and fish to feed myself, but when I place that basket in God's hands he will multiply it beyond what I can imagine. I don't need to know how it will all work out, I just need to have faith that it WILL.

"I prayed for healing on this side of Heaven, but instead I got peace. Layla got both."

Chapter 9

Fear Factor

Does anyone else remember the TV show from years ago called *Fear Factor*? The premise was to get a bunch of contestants doing crazy challenges, all designed to scare the pants off of them. The last man standing wins. The ones that always seemed the worst to me were the challenges involving insects or heights, which was basically all of them. I'll give a hard pass to lying in a glass coffin with eight million creepy crawly things all over me, thank you very much.

Most of us don't mind being a little bit scared. Haunted houses, roller coasters, opening the electric bill in the middle of summer in Texas . . . all designed to give us "safe" scares. Statistically, you probably won't die or get maimed from these activities, but our brains tell us it's fun to live on the edge. Oh, and scary movies! Those were my favorite growing up. I remember when *The Blair Witch Project* came out between my freshman and sophomore years of college, and I thought it was awesome. But if I try to watch movies like that now, where they're filmed from a first-person perspective, I get nauseous. Also, is it just me, or have horror movies really started going over the top these days? Do we really need seven movies in the *Saw* franchise? I feel like one would have been sufficient.

I loved all that stuff when I was a kid, but now, I'm more of a merry-go-round girl. Give me something safe over scary, please and thank you. Something happens in your brain when you become a parent. Some switch is flipped and all of a sudden you're able to see danger all around. A seemingly innocent grape is now a choking hazard, and the cord on the blinds is just waiting to hang your small child. And once you know things, you can't un-know them. I haven't watched an episode of *Law & Order SVU* since having kids. Sorry, Mariska Hargitay, but I don't need extra help in imagining the thousands of terrible things that can happen to kids in real life. I'm a mom and I can make that stuff up in my own head.

The thing about fear is that it's a real, living thing. The more we feed it, the more it grows and the stronger it becomes. When we sit and dwell on negative thoughts, they begin to take over the good thoughts like a parasite. Fear and anxiety need those bad thoughts to exist.

So how do we overcome them? The best way is by not giving them a foothold in the first place, which of course is easier said than done. The second way, I've found, is to be prepared. Much like a woman carries pepper spray in her purse, when we carry our faith and trust in the Lord we can fight off the enemy. If a bad thought jumps in, faith recognizes the intruder and kicks it out.

> **They will have no fear of bad news; their hearts are steadfast, trusting the Lord. (Psalm 112:7)**

Did you know I had never heard the term "the enemy" until a few years ago? At least, not in the context of "the enemy" being Satan, but it made total sense to me. We live our lives under a constant mental attack from Satan and his goons. He's a sneaky bastard who is very in tune with what makes each of us tick. The bad news is he doesn't need much room to shove his way in and escalate one small fear or anxious thought all the way to crazy town. The good news is that he's highly unoriginal. He works from the same playbook again and again because he knows what gets the job done (ok, so he's efficient and unoriginal), but that makes him super easy to spot. Like, seriously easy once you know what you're looking for. All you need is light.

> **Our deceiver operates in the darkness. And he hopes we will, too. As long as we're stumbling around shrouded in darkness-not really sure what's true and what's not—we'll never be able to see him for who he really is and detect the underlying intentions of his plans. What we need is a spotlight that pierces the darkness and lays bare all his evil schemes, systems, and illusions. The truth of God's Word is that light! (Pricilla Shirer,** *Armor of God*)[13]

Priscilla Shirer describes the devil's intentions and M-O to a tee here. I could basically quote her entire *Armor of God* book in this chapter (it would be a long one), but instead I will highly recommend you pick up a copy and read it.

I mentioned in a previous chapter that I was once an apocalyptic worrier, but now I know exactly where all that worrying came from—the enemy. I allowed myself to go down rabbit holes filled with fear and anxiety, and Satan was happy to tag along. Pretty soon, he was throwing carrot sticks and waiting for me to chase after them. After a while, it becomes extraordinarily difficult to discern what's real and what isn't.

That's where our relationship with God becomes important. It takes time and practice to know the difference between God's and the enemy's voice when you've been surrounded by the enemy for so long, but I'll give you a tip. The Bible tells us that God has not given us a spirit of fear (2 Timothy 1:7). That's it. That's my shortcut for knowing whether or not my thoughts are of God.

My gut is like a barometer of discernment (that's a weird thought, isn't it, but it's so true). If I'm dwelling on a thought that leaves my gut feeling icky with fear or worry, it's highly likely that the enemy is playing around in my head. On the flip side, if I've got butterflies and feel excitement (even if the thought still seems a little scary), I'm more inclined to believe it's from God.

For example, whenever I had thoughts about writing this book and what that could look like for other people, my stomach got all excited and topsy-turvey. I imagined the lives it could impact and the people who need to hear His message through our story. The other side of that is when I begin having anxious feelings about how hard it will be to get published, or the fact that there's already sooooo many Christian authors out there—people I admire like Jen Hatmaker, Melanie Shankle, or Jennie Allen, who might look at my work and laugh. *Who does she think she is*, I imagine they'll say. All those thoughts, Satan has produced. I have to physically shake myself out of that trance and remember that my story is different than their stories. What I have to share is unique, and God has shown me the people who are suffering deeply in their need for control. This book is for them.

Most of the time, it's easier to try and ignore the fear. If we knew the actual problem, then we'd be forced to address it. As long as we pretend it's not there, it's fine. Unfortunately, the problems don't really go away, they just get more inflamed under the surface. I think of it like my computer when it's not acting the way I want it to. I have a Mac and if there's an application that isn't working or needs my attention, the icon will hop up and down. It's truly annoying when you're right in the middle of something important. I scold the icon and tell it to stop. I'll get to you later, I tell it, but there it goes again. It hop, hop, hops until I give it the attention it wants. If I were to ignore it indefinitely, the whole computer would start to slow down. By the time you get to that point, you're not even sure what's causing the problem because all the applications have started to act funky. So, what do you do? We reboot of course! That's the solution you'd get from any highly trained tech person when you call the Help Desk.

Have you ever tried rebooting your life? Much like my computer, the issues surface innocently, politely asking for attention. As we continue to ignore them, they slowly begin to impact other areas of our lives. When we're stuck in the middle of it, we have no idea what to do. If I go back and try to figure out what the original problem was, I'll see two or three things that went wrong. What now? Which issue gets attention first?

In cases like these we often need a reboot ourselves, but what does that look like? There's no round little button on my life that lets me turn it off and back on again. For some people, taking a vacation, changing jobs, or moving can be considered a reboot. (Spoiler alert: the problems you left behind are still waiting for you.) The big ones tend to stick around. Instead of ignoring or being afraid to see what the problem is, it's time to set aside our need to control the diagnosis and just ask God to reveal to us the root cause. He's more than capable of pointing out which application is taking up space and causing everything else to be out of whack.

In my own life, what gets pointed out to me is my desire for control (shocker, right?). That control can come in many different packages, but when those trappings are examined thoroughly, it's the real root cause. For some, it's a dependency on substances, shopping, or eating, when there should be a dependency on Christ. These are the three biggest issues I see plaguing our culture most of the time, but there are so many more. The thing they all have in common is that they're a poor substitute for what we're really searching for. We begin feeling weighed down by all the problems life throws at us. Once we surrender, we begin to view them in a different light. The weight is lifted and He makes our feet like those of a deer, enabling us to tread on the heights (Habakkuk 3:19).

Have you ever thought about when we start becoming susceptible to Satan's tricks? Is there an age at which we become eligible for his work? Is it a life milestone, like getting your driver's license? Sadly, no. I do think our children are more in tune with God's voice at a young age, which serves as a protection for them. Now, please keep in mind, this is all anecdotal because I have zero experience in child psychology or any other fancy degree. I was always in complete awe of how brave and steadfast Layla was during treatment. All of those kids are. There is still fear there, but to see the way they adapt and adjust once it passes is amazing to me.

One of the things nurses and doctors had to do regularly was access Layla's port for medication. If you're not familiar with that term (first, thank your lucky stars you aren't), a port is a device that is implanted right under the skin, usually in the chest or side area. It's directly connected to a large vein with a soft tube called a catheter. By "accessing" the port, a patient can receive medication, blood transfusions, or even have blood drawn. It does result in fewer pokes overall, but there are downsides. The cleaning process prior to access is rigorous due to the high risk of infection. A person can easily get a blood infection if any bacteria or germs make their way inside. A blood infection is serious business—it equals long hospital stays and is no fun. Now that you're up to speed, you might have a better understanding of why the process of accessing a port is traumatic for many kids, especially little ones. Everyone in the room wears a mask and the patient needs to stay very still. If anyone touches the area being cleaned, you start all over.

Our routine generally consisted of Layla sitting on my lap, with both of us lifting her shirt up to cover her mouth and nose. This exposed her chest for port access, but also helped serve as her mask. She hated wearing the Mickey Mouse masks provided because she said they were stinky. This position also allowed me to hold her arms still when she got wiggly. Our wonderful child-life specialist would be in the room, helping by distracting her with the iPad or whatever else we could think of. No matter how much we talked about the process and tried to prepare her for it, the fear eventually took over. She couldn't help it. After it was all done, she'd calm down and say, "I tried to be brave, Mommy." She was always brave in my mind, but the fear was out of her control. It had become a Pavlovian response to her surroundings.

Each time we visited the hospital, Layla would ask if we had to "do port" that day. I loved the days that I could tell her, "Nope! Not today, Bug!" But my heart sank on the yes days. From the moment she realized what would happen that day, you could see her mental state start to change. She was less talkative and more shy. Satan had started his work. She knew it wasn't that painful in reality because we used a numbing cream, but the whole process and the requirement to be still triggered her anxiety. It was a direct reflection of the fact that she had no control over her circumstances at the time. That's really the kicker for all of it, isn't it? We fear the lack of control.

So, how do we remove ourselves from Satan's grasp? My experience has shown me that you can't outrun or hide from him. He'll find you and has no problem attacking from your blind side. The key is standing in faith in front of him, even when everything in your being wants you to run.

Our pastor told a story the other day that had me saying, "Yes! This is exactly what it feels like to be drowning in grief!" The story was about a trip he took on his sabbatical. He's an avid hiker and was visiting a beautiful spot in Canada. He was on his way to the airport and decided to stop along the way for a hike. But he got to the trailhead and was held back by two signs. One talked about wolves and what to do if they approached you, the other was about bears. Both signs indicated, emphatically, that you SHOULD NOT RUN if you encounter either of these animals. Can you imagine? Minding your own business while on a lovely hike and crossing paths with a bear? Now I'm not sure exactly which types of bears frequent that particular location, but a bear is a bear, and I'm fairly certain my instincts would be telling me to R-U-N! Don't look back and go! It would be futile, of course, because bears can run like thirty miles an hour, and once you start running they take that as an invitation to have lunch (with you as the main course).

> It's so hard to stand your ground when everything in you wants to run.
>
> (Pete Briscoe)

That's a lot like how it feels to confront Satan in the midst of the chaos he's created. Your instincts are to run, to find cover in the storm, but we must be still. When we stand firm in our faith, we are telling the enemy that our trust in our Savior far outweighs the fear we feel. When we look Satan in the face and say, "I'm not falling for it, Buster," we take away his power. Even though we may not see Him, our Heavenly Father has us surrounded like an invisible force field when we activate our trust and faith in Him. We cannot be destroyed.

> **They are brought to their knees and fall, but we rise up and stand firm.**
>
> **(Psalm 20:8)**

Eventually we had to make the decision to stop treatment and enjoy whatever time we had left with Layla. Her decline happened quickly, which Bryan and I both felt was a blessing and a curse, but the one thing I'll always remember is Layla's peace. She had the peace of being at home, cozy on the couch or in her own bed. No pokes and no needles, only medicine to keep her comfortable and free from pain. We were with her constantly and so was the Holy Spirit. It was a tangible presence in our home.

There were times when we could tell Layla wasn't quite with us, even before she passed. I would often ask her if she went away for a while and she'd nod her head yes. I would ask if it was a nice place and she'd nod her head yes again. Then I'd always ask her if she had seen Jesus and she'd shake her head no. "If you see Him," I would tell her, "it's ok for you to go with Him. Jesus loves you just like Mommy and Daddy." She would nod her head yes. She knew. Even at five years old, she had an intimate relationship with her Heavenly Father. She wasn't afraid to go, it just wasn't quite time.

After her death, I wanted nothing more than to follow her, but that's not an option for those of us stuck here on earth. It still seems appealing on the days I can't seem to pull myself up out of the sadness, but Layla has a daddy and a brother and a baby sister who all need each other here. Ah . . . there's the rub. Those who remain behind get the short end of the stick. If we know our loved ones are in Heaven, then we know they are free from pain and any ailments that plagued them in life. The rest of us are left to navigate life and grief. Layla doesn't spend her days in Heaven missing her family, which I'll admit hurts a little, but mostly it brings me great joy. Now, our tears are the only ones that get shed.

Daily, people still tell me they don't know how I do it. How do I function or even smile? I'll share a little secret with you—I'm not afraid. I'm not afraid to feel sad or to talk about our daughter, even if it means I cry in front of a stranger. I'm not afraid of what the future holds for our family because I have seen what God can do even when the answered prayer doesn't come in the package I want.

Some days, it takes a change in perspective. I prayed for healing on this side of Heaven, but instead I got peace. Layla got both. This must be what the Bible is talking about in 1 James, where we're told to consider it pure joy when we face troubles. Our family faced an insurmountable mountain in front of us, but it wasn't permanent, and I learned so much in the process. I learned that I am strong only because He is. I am brave only because my faith is a supernatural weapon.

As I put Daniel to bed last night, he picked my favorite book to read for the one hundredth time. It's *Far Flutterby* by Karen Kingsbury and I never get tired of reading it. Little Cody the caterpillar sums faith up perfectly, so I'll leave you with his words:

"Have faith through the hard times, believing in more! For there in the journey and stuck in the sting, the struggle . . . the struggle . . . is what gives you WINGS!"[14]

Friend, there is nothing too big that you cannot trust God with. Let go of your desire for control, lean into the struggle, and yes, even the sting, and you will see the beauty He can create with it.

Citations

1   Sarah Young, "January 26" in *Jesus Calling* (Thomas Nelson, 2004), 27

2   Sarah Young, "January 28" in *Jesus Calling* (Thomas Nelson, 2004), 29

3   Quote from A.W. Tozer on page 17: R. Mark Dillon, *Giving and Getting in the Kingdom: A Field Guide*, (Moody Publishers, 2012

4   Karen Kingsbury, *Far Flutterby* (ZonderKidz, 2011)

5   "The Potentials of Faith", Chuck Smith: Sermon Notes for Matthew 17:20, https://www.blueletterbible.org/Comm/smith_chuck/SermonNotes_Mat/Mat_183.cfm

6   Beth More, "Five" in *The Quest: An Excursion Toward Intimacy with God* (LifeWay Press, 2017), 17

7   Sarah Young, "January 25" in *Jesus Calling* (Thomas Nelson, 2004), 26

8   Priscilla Shirer, "Week One" in *Armor of God* (LifeWay Press, 2015), 11

9   Beth More, "Four" in *The Quest: An Excursion Toward Intimacy with God* (LifeWay Press, 2017), 127

10 Beth More, "Four" in *The Quest: An Excursion Toward Intimacy with God* (LifeWay Press, 2017), 128

11 Louie Giglio, "Life is Short, God is Big" in *Goliath Must Fall: Winning the Battle Against Your Giants* (Thomas Nelson, 2017), 130

12 Jennie Allen, *Proven: Where Christ's Abundance Meets Our Great Need* (LifeWay Press, 2017)

13 Priscilla Shirer, "Week Two" in *Armor of God* (LifeWay Press, 2015), 58

14 Karen Kingsbury, *Far Flutterby* (ZonderKidz, 2011)

Acknowledgments

I consider this book to be my fourth child. A child I was pregnant with for roughly fifteen months, but one that was living within me for years just waiting for the right time to be planted. Like every pregnancy, this one had its pain points. The times when I found it hard to sleep or eat because all I wanted to do was write, I could literally feel the Holy Spirit within me whispering the words He wanted me to write.

Other times I would sit at the computer and cry ugly tears, asking God "why?" Why did I need to write this book at all? Why couldn't this be someone else's story to tell? His answer—"Why not you?" His answer was not you're-not-exempt-from-suffering, but you-are-able. Thank you to those who God used to remind me daily that I am able.

To my family, especially my dad. I learned my first lessons about faith from you and you continue to show me that we can develop and mature what faith means as we grow with Christ. To my friends, all of you who stood with us during Layla's cancer journey and continue to pray and care for us still. Our POPCS and Bent Tree families . . . there aren't words enough to cover the gratitude in my heart for you.

Thank you to everyone who read, pre-read, and re-read this book. Those who gave feedback and constructive criticism, I hope the final product makes you proud.

For Patti, Brandi, Marie, and Michelle H., our entire board of directors and advisory board . . . I love you for serving Layla's Legacy with all you have and for carrying on our girl's memory as if she were your own child.

Alexa, thank you for walking with me through this process. Without you this book would have never seen the light of day. God knew what He was doing when our paths crossed in that Facebook group years ago. You kept me on track when I was ready to pack it in.

For Dr. Bowers and Dr. Maher . . . thank you for your continued kindness and friendship far past the doctor/patient boundary. I believe we will see a day when you no longer have to tell parents their time with their child is limited because of the hard work you are doing.

Kristen P, Janelle, Kim D, Becca, Laura C, Shelby . . . my fellow mommies with angel babies. You ladies get it and I love you. Thank you for always being an ear to listen even though we are separated by many miles and states. I know our kiddos are watching us together in Heaven!

Most importantly, and above all else, thank you to my husband Bryan. Thank you for loving me in my ugliest and messiest moments and for being my partner through the unimaginable parts of life. I love you darling.

About the Author

Sara Stamp is the author of *The Other F-Word: When Faith Fills The Gap*. She is also the Executive Director of Layla's Legacy Foundation, an organization created to honor the memory of her daughter Layla, who passed away at the age of five from Medulloblastoma, a common form of pediatric brain cancer. Layla's Legacy raises money to fund research to cure pediatric brain cancer and to financially assist families impacted by the disease. Sara is passionate about connecting with others as an encourager during times of loss and grief, especially when it relates to cancer. "It's part of the healing process for me," she says.

Above all, she is a wife, mother, and friend. Sara lives in Dallas, Texas with her husband Bryan and two children, Daniel and Evelyn. You can connect with Sara through Layla's Legacy or The Other F-Word Blog:

www.SaraStamp.com
Facebook: www.Facebook.com/LaylasLegacy
Instagram: @sarabstamp @LaylasLegacy

35982787R00090

Made in the USA
Lexington, KY
09 April 2019